Atlantic Diet Meal Plan

Simple and Delicious Meal Plans for a Healthier You, Atlantic Meal plan| Meal cookbook + 7 DAYS MEAL PLAN

By

Darryl E. Hinrichs

Copyright © by Darryl E. Hinrichs 2024. All rights reserved.

Before this document is duplicated or reproduced in any manner, the publisher's consent must be gained. Therefore, the contents within can neither be stored electronically, transferred, nor kept in a database. Neither in Part nor full can the document be copied, scanned, faxed, or retained without approval from the publisher or creator.

TABLE OF CONTENTS

INTRODUCTION... 7
CHAPTER 1... **15**
Understanding the Atlantic Diet.. **15**
   Origin and History.. 15
   Key Principles and Guidelines... 18
CHAPTER 2... **21**
Getting Started with the Atlantic Diet................................ **21**
   Preparing Your Kitchen.. 21
   Shopping for Atlantic Diet-Friendly Foods..................... 25
CHAPTER 3... **31**
Atlantic Diet Meal Planning.. **31**
   Basic Principles of Meal Planning................................... 31
   7 Days Meal Plan... 36
   Sample Meal Plans for Different Dietary Needs............ 38
CHAPTER 4... **43**
ATLANTIC RECIPES... **43**
   BREAKFAST RECIPES... 43
   Lunch Recipes... 72
   Dinner Recipes.. 99
   Snack Recipes... 133
CHAPTER 5... **149**
Cooking Techniques for the Atlantic Diet......................... **149**
   Tips for Healthy Cooking... 149
   Kitchen Equipment Essentials for the Atlantic Diet..... 154
CHAPTER 6... **157**
Incorporating Atlantic Diet Principles into Your Lifestyle... **157**
   Dining Out on the Atlantic Diet....................................... 157
   Socializing and Celebrating with Atlantic Diet-Friendly Foods... 164
   Tips for Enjoying Social Events....................................... 167

CHAPTER 7.. 169
Maintaining Success on the Atlantic Diet.................169
   Staying Motivated.. 169
   Tips for overcoming common challenges................... 174
FAQs about the Atlantic Diet.................................. 177
CONCLUSION..183

INTRODUCTION

The Atlantic diet, rooted in the rich culinary traditions of countries bordering the Atlantic Ocean, offers a flavorful and healthful approach to eating. In this book, we explore the principles, foods, and benefits of the Atlantic diet, providing you with the tools and knowledge to embrace this lifestyle.

Overview of the Atlantic Diet

The Atlantic Diet represents a rich tapestry of culinary traditions from the coastlines of Portugal, Spain, France, and Scandinavia, each contributing unique flavors and practices to this wholesome dietary pattern. Rooted in the same principles as the Mediterranean diet, it prioritizes whole, unprocessed foods readily available across the diverse Atlantic regions.

At its core, this diet includes a bounty of fresh fruits and vegetables, whole grains, legumes, nuts, and seeds, with a particular emphasis on the wide variety of seafood caught off the Atlantic coasts. Olive oil is the cornerstone fat source, used in place of butter and other saturated fats, known for its heart-healthy fats and anti-inflammatory properties. Dairy is enjoyed in moderation, focusing on natural and artisanal products.

More than just a way of eating, the Atlantic Diet encapsulates a lifestyle. Meals are not only nourishing but also form a pivotal social experience, often shared with family and friends. This communal aspect underscores the diet's cultural and social significance, reinforcing its role in promoting not just physical health but also mental and social well-being.

The Atlantic Diet also emphasizes the importance of sustainable eating practices, advocating for local and seasonal food sourcing. This not only supports local economies but also reduces the environmental impact, aligning with a globally increasing awareness of food sustainability.

Health Benefits of the Atlantic Diet

The Atlantic diet is a traditional dietary pattern followed by people living in countries bordering the Atlantic Ocean, such as Portugal, Spain, France, and parts of the United Kingdom. This diet is characterized by its emphasis on fresh, seasonal, and locally sourced foods, including fish, seafood, fruits, vegetables, whole grains, nuts, and olive oil. Similar to the Mediterranean diet, the Atlantic diet has gained attention for its numerous health benefits. In this article, we will explore the health benefits of the Atlantic diet and why it's worth considering as part of a healthy lifestyle.

1. Rich in Nutrients

One of the key benefits of the Atlantic diet is that it is rich in essential nutrients. Fish and seafood, which are staple foods in this diet, are excellent sources of protein, omega-3 fatty acids, vitamins, and minerals. Omega-3 fatty acids, in particular, are known for their anti-inflammatory properties and are beneficial for heart health.

2. Heart-Healthy

Numerous studies have shown that the Atlantic diet can help reduce the risk of heart disease. The high intake of fish and seafood, which are rich in omega-3 fatty acids, has been linked to lower levels of cholesterol and triglycerides, as well as a reduced risk of developing heart disease.

3. Weight Management

The Atlantic diet is also beneficial for weight management. It emphasizes whole, nutrient-dense foods and limits processed and high-calorie foods. This can help promote satiety and prevent overeating, which may aid in weight loss and weight management.

4. Antioxidant-Rich

Fruits, vegetables, and olive oil, which are key components of the Atlantic diet, are rich in antioxidants. Antioxidants help protect the body against oxidative stress and inflammation, which are linked to various chronic diseases, including cancer and heart disease.

5. Supports Brain Health

The Atlantic diet is also beneficial for brain health. The omega-3 fatty acids found in fish and seafood are important for brain function and development. Studies have shown that a diet rich in omega-3 fatty acids may help improve memory, cognition, and mood.

6. Reduces Inflammation

Inflammation is a natural response of the immune system, but chronic inflammation can contribute to the development of various diseases, including heart disease, diabetes, and cancer. The Atlantic diet, with its focus on anti-inflammatory foods such as fish, olive oil, fruits, and vegetables, can help reduce inflammation in the body.

7. Improves Digestive Health

The Atlantic diet is also beneficial for digestive health. It includes a variety of fiber-rich foods, such as fruits, vegetables, and whole grains, which can help promote healthy digestion and prevent digestive issues such as constipation and bloating.

8. May Reduce the Risk of Chronic Diseases

Overall, the Atlantic diet is associated with a reduced risk of chronic diseases. Its emphasis on whole, nutrient-dense foods and its ability to reduce inflammation and oxidative stress in the body make it a valuable dietary pattern for promoting overall health and well-being.

The Atlantic diet offers a wide range of health benefits, from heart health to brain health to weight management. By incorporating the principles of the Atlantic diet into your own eating habits, you can improve your overall health and well-being.

CHAPTER 1

Understanding the Atlantic Diet

Origin and History

The Atlantic diet is not just a modern-day trend; it has deep roots in the history and culture of the regions surrounding the Atlantic Ocean. Understanding the origin and history of the Atlantic diet provides valuable insights into its principles and why it remains relevant today.

Origins of the Atlantic Diet

The Atlantic diet is a traditional dietary pattern that originated in countries bordering the Atlantic Ocean, including Portugal, Spain,

France, Ireland, the United Kingdom, and parts of Scandinavia. It is characterized by a high consumption of fresh fruits and vegetables, fish, seafood, whole grains, nuts, and olive oil, with moderate amounts of dairy, poultry, and red wine.

The diet is rooted in the agricultural practices and culinary traditions of these regions, which have been shaped by the climate, geography, and cultural influences over centuries. For example, the Mediterranean climate of southern Europe favors the cultivation of olive trees, which has led to the widespread use of olive oil in Mediterranean diets, including the Atlantic diet.

Historical Influences

The Atlantic diet has been influenced by various historical events and cultural exchanges over the centuries. One of the earliest influences was the Roman Empire, which introduced new crops and culinary techniques to the region, including the cultivation of olives and grapes for olive oil and wine production.

During the Middle Ages, trade and exploration brought new foods and flavors to Europe from Africa, Asia, and the Americas. The Columbian Exchange, initiated by Christopher Columbus's voyages to the Americas in the late 15th century, introduced foods like potatoes, tomatoes, corn, and beans to Europe, which eventually became staples of the Atlantic diet.

Traditional Practices and Customs

The Atlantic diet is not just about the foods people eat; it also encompasses the way meals are prepared, shared, and enjoyed. Traditional practices and customs play a significant role in the Atlantic diet, reflecting the cultural heritage of the region.

One such tradition is the Mediterranean custom of the "Mediterranean diet," where meals are often enjoyed with family and friends, emphasizing the social aspect of eating. Another tradition is the Portuguese "petiscos," which are small, tapas-like dishes that are shared among diners, encouraging a communal dining experience.

Evolution of the Atlantic Diet

While the core principles of the Atlantic diet have remained consistent over the years, it has also evolved in response to changing lifestyles, dietary trends, and food availability. For example, modern interpretations of the Atlantic diet may include more processed foods and less physical activity than traditional diets.

Despite these changes, the Atlantic diet continues to be celebrated for its health benefits and cultural significance. Its emphasis on fresh, whole foods and mindful eating practices make it a sustainable and enjoyable way of eating for people of all ages.

Key Principles and Guidelines

The Atlantic Diet is centered around several key principles that emphasize the consumption of whole, minimally processed foods:

- Plant-Based Foods: The diet is rich in fruits, vegetables, legumes, nuts, and whole grains, which provide a wide range of nutrients and fiber.

- Seafood: Seafood, particularly fish and shellfish, is a staple of the Atlantic Diet and is a rich source of protein, omega-3 fatty acids, and other essential nutrients.

- Olive Oil: Olive oil is the primary source of fat in the diet and is used for cooking and dressing foods. It is rich in monounsaturated fats and antioxidants.

- Moderate Dairy: Dairy products, such as cheese and yogurt, are consumed in moderation in the Atlantic Diet and provide calcium and protein.

- Limited Red Meat: Red meat is consumed sparingly in the Atlantic Diet, with a focus on lean cuts and smaller portions.

- Wine in Moderation: Wine is often consumed in moderation with meals in the Atlantic Diet and is believed to have health benefits when consumed in moderation.

The Atlantic Diet is more than just a way of eating; it is a reflection of the cultural and culinary heritage of the Atlantic coastal regions. By embracing the principles of the Atlantic Diet, you can not only improve your health but also connect with a rich tradition that has stood the test of time.

CHAPTER 2

Getting Started with the Atlantic Diet

Preparing Your Kitchen

Embarking on the Atlantic diet journey requires some preparation, particularly in your kitchen. Setting up your kitchen for success will make it easier to follow the Atlantic diet principles and prepare delicious meals.

The Atlantic diet emphasizes fresh, whole foods that are rich in nutrients and flavor. To successfully follow this diet, it's important to prepare your kitchen so that it supports your new eating habits. In this section, we'll discuss how to set up your kitchen for success on the Atlantic diet. Here's how you can get started:

Purge Your Pantry

Before you start stocking up on Atlantic diet-friendly foods, take some time to go through your pantry and refrigerator to get rid of any items that don't align with the Atlantic diet principles. This includes processed foods, sugary snacks, and high-fat items that are not part of the Atlantic diet.

Stock Up on Atlantic Diet Staples

The Atlantic diet is rich in fruits, vegetables, whole grains, and lean proteins. Make sure your kitchen is stocked with these staples so that you always have the ingredients you need to prepare healthy meals. Some staples to have on hand include:

- Fruits: Apples, berries, oranges, etc.
- Vegetables: Spinach, kale, tomatoes, peppers, etc.
- Whole grains: Brown rice, quinoa, oats, etc.

- Lean proteins: Chicken, fish, beans, lentils, etc.

Invest in Quality Cookware

Having the right cookware can make it easier to prepare healthy meals. Invest in high-quality pots, pans, and utensils that will last and make cooking more enjoyable. Non-stick pans, a good chef's knife, and a sturdy cutting board are essential items to have in your kitchen.

Organize Your Kitchen

A well-organized kitchen can make cooking and meal preparation more efficient. Keep your kitchen organized by storing similar items together, labeling containers, and keeping frequently used items within easy reach. This will help you stay on track with your Atlantic diet goals.

Create a Meal Plan and Shopping List

Planning your meals in advance can help you stay on track with the Atlantic diet. Create a weekly meal plan that includes breakfast, lunch, dinner, and snacks, and make a shopping list based on your plan. This will help you avoid impulse purchases and ensure that you have everything you need to prepare healthy meals.

Set Up a Meal Prep Station

Meal prepping can save you time and make it easier to stick to the Atlantic diet. Set up a designated area in your kitchen for meal prep, with containers for storing prepped ingredients and meals. Spend some time each week chopping vegetables, cooking grains, and preparing proteins so that you have healthy options ready to go.

Stay Inspired

Keeping your kitchen stocked with inspiring ingredients can motivate you to cook and eat healthy meals. Visit your local farmers' market or specialty grocery store to discover new and exciting ingredients that you can incorporate into your Atlantic diet recipes.

By preparing your kitchen for the Atlantic diet, you'll be setting yourself up for success on your journey to better health. With a well-stocked kitchen and a little planning, you'll find that following the Atlantic diet is not only delicious but also sustainable in the long run.

Shopping for Atlantic Diet-Friendly Foods

The Atlantic diet is a wholesome and nutritious way of eating that is inspired by the culinary traditions of countries bordering the Atlantic Ocean. It emphasizes fresh, locally sourced ingredients and is rich in seafood, whole grains, fruits, vegetables, nuts, and olive oil. Shopping for Atlantic Diet-friendly foods involves selecting high-quality, nutrient-dense ingredients that form the foundation of this healthy eating pattern. In this guide, we'll explore the key components of the Atlantic diet and provide tips on how to shop for and incorporate these foods into your diet.

1. Understanding the Atlantic Diet

Before you start shopping, it's important to understand the key principles of the Atlantic diet. This diet is based on the traditional eating habits of countries like Portugal, Spain, France, and Italy, where fresh, seasonal, and locally sourced foods are central to the culinary culture. The Atlantic diet emphasizes:

- Seafood: Fish and seafood are staples of the Atlantic diet, providing protein, omega-3 fatty acids, and other essential nutrients.
- Whole Grains: Whole grains like oats, barley, and whole wheat are important sources of fiber, vitamins, and minerals in the Atlantic diet.
- Fruits and Vegetables: These should make up a large portion of your diet, providing antioxidants, vitamins, and minerals.
- Nuts and Seeds: These are good sources of healthy fats, protein, and fiber, and are often used in cooking and baking.
- Olive Oil: Olive oil is the primary source of fat in the Atlantic diet, providing heart-healthy monounsaturated fats and antioxidants.

2. Making a Shopping List

Before heading to the store, make a list of Atlantic Diet-friendly foods you'll need for the week. This will help you stay organized and avoid impulse purchases. Your list should include:

- Fresh Produce: Include a variety of fruits and vegetables, aiming for a rainbow of colors to ensure you're getting a wide range of nutrients.
- Seafood: Choose a variety of fish and seafood, including oily fish like salmon, mackerel, and sardines, which are rich in omega-3s.
- Whole Grains: Stock up on whole grains like oats, barley, brown rice, and whole wheat pasta.
- Nuts and Seeds: Include a variety of nuts and seeds, such as almonds, walnuts, chia seeds, and flaxseeds, for snacking and cooking.
- Olive Oil: Opt for extra virgin olive oil, which is the least processed and retains the most nutrients and flavor.

3. Shopping Tips

When shopping for Atlantic Diet-friendly foods, keep these tips in mind:

- Buy Local and Seasonal: Choose locally sourced and seasonal foods whenever possible. Not only are they fresher, but they also support local farmers and are often more affordable.
- Read Labels: Check labels for added sugars, unhealthy fats, and other undesirable ingredients. Choose products with minimal processing and natural ingredients.
- Stock Up on Staples: Keep your pantry stocked with staples like whole grains, canned fish, olive oil, and spices, so you can easily whip up a healthy meal.
- Try New Foods: Be adventurous and try new foods that are common in Atlantic cuisine but may be less familiar to you. This can help keep your diet interesting and varied.
- Plan Ahead: Take some time to plan your meals for the week based on the foods you've purchased. This can help you make healthier choices and reduce food waste.

4. Meal Prep Ideas

Once you've shopped for your Atlantic Diet-friendly foods, consider doing some meal prep to make healthy eating easier throughout the week. Here are some ideas:

- Prep Vegetables: Wash, chop, and store vegetables in the fridge so they're ready to use in salads, stir-fries, and other dishes.
- Cook Grains: Cook a batch of whole grains like quinoa or brown rice and store them in the fridge for quick and easy meals.
- Marinate Fish: Marinate fish fillets in olive oil, lemon juice, and herbs before storing them in the fridge or freezer for later use.
- Make Soups and Stews: Prepare a large batch of soup or stew with plenty of vegetables, beans, and lean protein for a hearty and nutritious meal.

Shopping for Atlantic Diet-friendly foods doesn't have to be daunting. By understanding the key principles of the Atlantic diet, making a shopping list, following shopping tips, and doing some meal prep, you can easily incorporate this healthy eating pattern into your lifestyle. With a little planning and preparation, you'll be well on your way to enjoying the delicious flavors and health benefits of the Atlantic diet.

CHAPTER 3

Atlantic Diet Meal Planning

Basic Principles of Meal Planning

Meal planning is a key aspect of maintaining a healthy and balanced diet. It involves choosing and preparing meals ahead of time to ensure you have nutritious and delicious options available when you need them. In this chapter, we will explore the basic principles of meal planning and how you can use them to create a meal plan that works for you.

Why Meal Planning Is Important

Meal planning offers several benefits, including:

- Saves Time: Planning your meals in advance can save you time during the week by reducing the need to decide what to eat each day.

- Saves Money: Meal planning can help you save money by allowing you to buy ingredients in bulk and avoid impulse purchases.

- Promotes Healthier Eating: By planning your meals, you can ensure you are eating a balanced diet with the right mix of nutrients.

- Reduces Food Waste: Meal planning can help you reduce food waste by buying only what you need and using leftovers in creative ways.

The Basic Steps of Meal Planning

- Set Your Goals: Start by setting your meal planning goals. Are you looking to eat healthier, save time, or stick to a budget?

- Choose Your Recipes: Select recipes that align with your goals and preferences. Consider factors like cooking time, ingredients, and dietary restrictions.

- Make a Shopping List: Based on your chosen recipes, create a shopping list of all the ingredients you will need for the week.

- Shop Smart: When shopping, stick to your list to avoid impulse purchases. Look for sales and discounts to save money.

- Prep Ahead: Take some time to prep ingredients ahead of time, such as chopping vegetables or marinating meat. This can save you time during the week.

- Cook in Batches: Consider cooking in batches and freezing meals for later. This can save you time and ensure you always have a healthy meal on hand.

- Stay Flexible: Be flexible with your meal plan. If something comes up and you can't stick to your plan, don't stress. Simply adjust and move on.

Tips for Successful Meal Planning

- Start Small: If you're new to meal planning, start with just a few days at a time. Once you get the hang of it, you can plan for a full week.

- Use What You Have: Before you start planning, take inventory of what you already have in your pantry and fridge. This can help you avoid buying duplicate items.

- Plan for Leftovers: Embrace leftovers and plan to use them in creative ways, such as turning last night's chicken into a sandwich for lunch.

- Get the Whole Family Involved: If you're planning meals for your family, get everyone involved in the process. This can help ensure everyone's preferences are taken into account.

- Stay Organized: Keep your meal plan and shopping list organized and easily accessible. Consider using a meal planning app or calendar to help you stay on track.

Meal planning is a valuable tool for anyone looking to eat healthier, save time, and reduce food waste. By following the basic principles outlined in this chapter, you can create a meal plan that works for you and your lifestyle. Experiment with different recipes and meal planning strategies to find what works best for you, and don't be afraid to adapt your plan as needed. With a little planning and preparation, you can enjoy delicious and nutritious meals every day.

7 Days Meal Plan

All Recipes and process for Preparing them will be later discussed in the guide

Day 1
Breakfast: Smoked Salmon and Avocado Toast
Lunch: Grilled Salmon Salad
Dinner: Grilled Salmon with Lemon and Dill
Snacks: Olive Tapenade, Greek Yogurt with Honey and Almonds

Day 2
Breakfast: Atlantic Omelette with Spinach and Feta
Lunch: Tuna and White Bean Salad
Dinner: Atlantic Fish Stew
Snacks: Tuna Stuffed Avocado, Baked Sweet Potato Chips

Day 3
Breakfast: Whole Grain Blueberry Pancakes
Lunch: Shrimp and Vegetable Stir-Fry
Dinner: Atlantic Diet Shrimp and Vegetable Stir-Fry
Snacks: Smoked Salmon Cucumber Bites, Roasted Red Pepper Hummus

Day 4
Breakfast: Greek Yogurt Parfait with Honey and Almonds
Lunch: Grilled Vegetable Wrap
Dinner: Cod with Tomato and Olive Sauce
Snacks: Grilled Zucchini Roll-Ups, Mediterranean Chickpea Salad

Day 5
Breakfast: Atlantic Salmon Breakfast Bowl
Lunch: Smoked Salmon and Avocado Sandwich
Dinner: Atlantic Diet Clam and Vegetable Pasta
Snacks: Sardine Pate, Apple Slices with Almond Butter

Day 6
Breakfast: Mediterranean Egg Muffins
Lunch: Lentil and Vegetable Soup
Dinner: Atlantic Diet Baked Stuffed Peppers
Snacks: Olive Tapenade, Greek Yogurt with Honey and Almonds

Day 7
Breakfast: Banana-Oat Blender Pancakes
Lunch: Quinoa and Black Bean Salad
Dinner: Atlantic Diet Seafood Paella
Snacks: Smoked Salmon Cucumber Bites, Baked Sweet Potato Chips

Feel free to swap meals and snacks to suit your preferences and schedule. Enjoy your Atlantic-inspired meals!

Sample Meal Plans for Different Dietary Needs

Vegetarian Meal Plan

Day 1:

Breakfast: Greek yogurt with honey and mixed berries

Snack: Carrot sticks with hummus

Lunch: Quinoa salad with chickpeas, cucumber, and feta cheese

Snack: Apple slices with almond butter

Dinner: Lentil soup with a side of whole grain bread

Day 2:

Breakfast: Oatmeal with almond milk, banana, and cinnamon

Snack: Greek yogurt with granola

Lunch: Spinach and feta omelet with a side of whole grain toast

Snack: Mixed nuts

Dinner: Vegetable stir-fry with tofu and brown rice

Day 3:

Breakfast: Smoothie with spinach, banana, almond milk, and protein powder

Snack: Rice cakes with avocado

Lunch: Lentil and vegetable stew

Snack: Greek yogurt with honey

Dinner: Eggplant parmesan with a side salad

Gluten-Free Meal Plan

Day 1:

Breakfast: Gluten-free toast with avocado and tomato

Snack: Rice cakes with almond butter

Lunch: Quinoa salad with grilled chicken, avocado, and lemon dressing

Snack: Mixed nuts

Dinner: Grilled salmon with quinoa and steamed vegetables

Day 2:

Breakfast: Gluten-free pancakes with maple syrup and berries

Snack: Greek yogurt with honey

Lunch: Turkey and avocado wrap with gluten-free tortilla

Snack: Rice cakes with hummus

Dinner: Baked chicken with sweet potato and green beans

Day 3:

Breakfast: Smoothie bowl with gluten-free granola and mixed berries

Snack: Rice cakes with almond butter

Lunch: Quinoa stuffed bell peppers

Snack: Mixed nuts

Dinner: Grilled shrimp with quinoa and roasted vegetables

Low-Carb Meal Plan

Day 1:

Breakfast: Scrambled eggs with spinach and feta cheese

Snack: Cottage cheese with cucumber slices

Lunch: Chicken Caesar salad with no croutons

Snack: Beef jerky

Dinner: Grilled steak with asparagus and a side salad

Day 2:

Breakfast: Greek yogurt with mixed berries and almonds

Snack: Celery sticks with cream cheese

Lunch: Turkey and cheese roll-ups with lettuce

Snack: Hard-boiled eggs

Dinner: Baked salmon with broccoli and cauliflower rice

Day 3:

Breakfast: Omelet with mushrooms, onions, and cheese

Snack: String cheese

Lunch: Tuna salad lettuce wraps

Snack: Almonds

Dinner: Grilled chicken with zucchini noodles and marinara sauce

CHAPTER 4

ATLANTIC RECIPES

BREAKFAST RECIPES

Welcome to the heart of your morning—Where nutrition meets gusto to kickstart your day! Breakfast isn't just the first meal of the day; it's the foundation of daily energy and a chance to infuse your body with essential nutrients. In this section, we explore a variety of Atlantic Diet-inspired recipes that promise not only to satisfy your taste buds but also to align with your health goals. Each recipes is crafted to offer a balanced, flavorful, and energizing start to your day. Whether you're sitting down to a leisurely breakfast or grabbing a quick bite on your way out, these dishes are designed to be simple, nutritious, and delightful. So, let's embrace the morning with vibrant foods that power our bodies and spirits!

Smoked Salmon and Avocado Toast

Nutritional Value(Per Servings): Calories: Approx 300-350 calories | Protein: 15-20 grams | Fat: 20-25 grams Carbohydrates: 20-30 grams | Fiber: 5-7 grams

Total Cook Time: 10 minutes

Servings: 2

Ingredients:

2 slices of whole grain bread

1 ripe avocado

4 slices of smoked salmon

1 tablespoon of lemon juice

Salt and black pepper to taste

Optional toppings: capers, red onion slices, fresh dill, or a sprinkle of crushed red pepper flakes

Instructions:

Toast the Bread:

Toast the bread slices to your preferred level of crispiness.

Prepare the Avocado Spread:

Peel and pit the avocado. In a small bowl, mash the avocado with the lemon juice until it reaches a smooth consistency.

Season with salt and pepper to taste.

Assemble the Toast:

Spread the mashed avocado evenly on each slice of toasted bread.

Lay two slices of smoked salmon on top of the avocado on each toast.

If desired, add any of the optional toppings like capers, thin slices of red onion, fresh dill, or a light sprinkle of red pepper flakes for extra flavor and texture.

Serve:

Serve immediately while the toast is still warm and crisp.

Nutritional Benefits: This breakfast is rich in omega-3 fatty acids from the salmon, which are beneficial for heart health. Avocado provides healthy fats, fiber, and various vitamins and minerals.

Atlantic Omelette with Spinach and Feta

Nutritional Value(Per Servings): Calories: Approx 300 calories | Protein: 18 grams | Fat: 23 grams Carbohydrates: 6 grams | Fiber:1 grams | Sodium: 400mg

Total Cook Time: 15 minutes

Servings: 2

Ingredients:

4 large eggs

2 cups fresh spinach, washed and roughly chopped

1/2 cup feta cheese, crumbled

1 small onion, finely chopped

2 tablespoons olive oil

Salt and pepper to taste

Optional: Fresh herbs (such as dill or parsley), chopped for garnish

Instructions:

Prepare Ingredients:

Heat 1 tablespoon of olive oil in a non-stick frying pan over medium heat.

Add the chopped onion and sauté until translucent, about 3-4 minutes.

Add the spinach to the pan and cook until it wilts,

approximately 2 minutes. Remove from heat.

Mix Eggs:

In a bowl, whisk the eggs with salt and pepper until well combined.

Stir in the cooked spinach and onion mixture along with the crumbled feta cheese.

Cook Omelette:

Heat the remaining tablespoon of olive oil in the same frying pan over medium heat.

Pour the egg mixture into the pan, spreading evenly.

Cook for about 4-5 minutes, or until the edges start to lift from the pan. Use a spatula to gently fold the omelette in half, and continue cooking for another 1-2 minutes until it is fully set.

Serve:

Carefully slide the omelette onto a plate, garnish with fresh herbs if using, and serve immediately.

Nutritional Benefits: This omelette is packed with protein from the eggs and calcium from the feta cheese. Spinach adds vitamins A and C, as well as iron

Whole Grain Blueberry Pancakes

Nutritional Value(Per Servings): Calories: Approx 280 kcal | Protein: 9 grams | Fat: 10 grams Carbohydrates: 40 grams | Fiber:5 grams | Sodium: 300mg

Total Cook Time: 30minutes

Servings: 4 (2 Pancakes Per Servings)

Ingredients:

1 cup whole wheat flour

1/2 cup oat flour

2 tablespoons honey or pure maple syrup

2 teaspoons baking powder

1/2 teaspoon salt

1 cup milk

2 large eggs

1/4 cup natural yogurt or applesauce (for added moisture)

2 tablespoons melted unsalted butter or coconut oil

1 teaspoon vanilla extract

1 cup fresh blueberries (more for serving if desired)

Cooking spray or additional butter for the pan

Instructions:

Mix Dry Ingredients: In a large bowl, whisk together whole wheat flour, oat flour, baking powder, and salt.

Combine Wet Ingredients: In another bowl, beat the eggs with the milk, yogurt or applesauce, melted butter, vanilla extract, and honey or maple syrup until smooth.

Combine Mixtures: Pour the wet ingredients into the dry ingredients and stir until just combined. Be careful not to overmix; some lumps are okay.

Add Blueberries: Gently fold the blueberries into the batter.

Heat the Pan: Heat a non-stick skillet or griddle over medium heat. Lightly grease with cooking spray or a dab of butter.

Cook Pancakes: Pour about 1/4 cup of batter for each pancake onto the hot skillet. Cook for 2-3 minutes on one side until bubbles form on the surface, then flip and cook for another 1-2 minutes on the other side until golden brown and cooked through.

Serve: Serve warm with additional blueberries and maple syrup or honey if desired.

Nutritional Benefits: These pancakes are made with whole grains, which provide fiber and B vitamins. Blueberries are rich in antioxidants and add natural sweetness.

Greek Yogurt Parfait with Honey and Almonds

Nutritional Value(Per Servings): Calories: Approx 450-500 kcal | Protein:22g grams | Fat: 18 grams Carbohydrates: 55 grams | Fiber: 5 grams | Sugar: 35g

Total Cook Time: 10 minutes

Servings: 2

Ingredients:

2 cups Greek yogurt

4 tablespoons honey

1/2 cup granola

1/2 cup almonds, roughly chopped (toasted for extra flavor)

1 cup mixed berries (such as blueberries, strawberries, and raspberries)

Instructions:

Prepare the Ingredients:

Wash the berries and slice any larger ones, such as strawberries, to ensure even layers.

If not already toasted, lightly toast the chopped almonds in a dry skillet over medium heat until they are golden and fragrant. Set aside to cool.

Assemble the Parfait:

In a glass or a parfait cup, layer 1/4 cup of Greek yogurt at the bottom.

Drizzle about 1 tablespoon of honey over the yogurt.

Add a layer of granola followed by a layer of mixed berries.

Sprinkle a portion of the toasted almonds on top.

Repeat the layering process until all ingredients are used up, finishing with a few berries and almonds on top for presentation.

Serve Immediately:

Serve the parfait immediately to enjoy the crunch of the granola, or refrigerate for up to an hour before serving to allow the flavors to meld together.

Nutritional Benefits:

Greek yogurt is high in protein and probiotics, which are beneficial for gut health. Almonds provide healthy fats and fiber, while berries are rich in antioxidants

Atlantic Salmon Breakfast Bowl

Nutritional Value(Per Servings): Calories: Approx 650 kcal | Protein:64g grams | Fat: 46 grams Carbohydrates: 32 grams | Fiber: 7 grams | Sugar: 3g

Cook Time: 20 minutes| Preparation Time: 10 minutes

Servings: 2

Ingredients:

2 fillets of Atlantic salmon (about 4 ounces each)

1 cup of cooked quinoa

1 avocado, sliced

1 cup of fresh spinach

1 small cucumber, sliced

4 radishes, thinly sliced

2 tablespoons of olive oil

1 lemon, juiced

Salt and pepper to taste

Fresh dill or parsley for garnish

Optional: 2 eggs (poached or soft boiled)

Dressing:

3 tablespoons olive oil

1 tablespoon lemon juice

1 teaspoon Dijon mustard

1 small clove garlic, minced

Salt and pepper to taste

Instructions:

Prepare the Salmon:

Preheat a non-stick skillet over medium heat and add one tablespoon of olive oil.

Season the salmon fillets with salt and pepper and place them skin-side down in the skillet.

Cook for about 6-7 minutes on the skin side until the skin is crisp. Flip the fillets and cook for an additional 3-4 minutes or until the salmon is cooked through and flakes easily with a fork. Remove from the skillet and set aside to cool slightly.

Make the Dressing:

In a small bowl, whisk together olive oil, lemon juice, Dijon mustard, minced garlic, salt, and pepper until emulsified.

Assemble the Bowl:

Divide the cooked quinoa between two bowls.

Arrange the spinach, sliced avocado, cucumber, and radishes around the quinoa.

Flake the salmon and add it to the bowl.

If using, top each bowl with a poached or soft-boiled egg.

Serve:

Drizzle the dressing over each bowl.

Garnish with fresh dill or parsley and a squeeze of lemon juice for extra freshness.

Season with additional salt and pepper to taste.

Nutritional Benefits: This breakfast bowl is rich in protein from the salmon and quinoa, as well as healthy fats from the avocado. It's also packed with vitamins and minerals from the vegetables.

Mediterranean Egg Muffins

Nutritional Value(Per Servings): Calories: Approx 100 | Protein:7 grams |Fat:7g

Carbohydrates: 3grams | Fiber: 0.5 grams | Sugar: 1.5g

Cook Time: 20 minutes| Prep Time: 10 minutes

Servings: 12 muffins

Ingredients:

10 large eggs

1/2 cup milk (any kind)

1 cup chopped spinach

1/2 cup diced bell peppers (mix of red, green, or yellow)

1/4 cup chopped onions

1/2 cup crumbled feta cheese

1/4 cup chopped Kalamata olives

1/2 teaspoon salt

1/4 teaspoon black pepper

1 teaspoon dried oregano

Cooking spray or oil, for greasing

Instructions:

Preheat the Oven and Prepare Muffin Tin:

Preheat your oven to 375°F (190°C). Grease a 12-cup muffin tin with cooking spray or a little oil to prevent sticking.

Mix Eggs and Milk:

In a large bowl, whisk together the eggs and milk until well combined.

Add Vegetables and Cheese:

Stir in the spinach, bell peppers, onions, feta cheese, and Kalamata olives into the egg mixture. Season with salt, pepper, and dried oregano.

Fill Muffin Cups:

Evenly distribute the egg mixture among the prepared muffin cups. Each cup should be about 3/4 full.

Bake:

Bake in the preheated oven for 20-25 minutes, or until the egg muffins are firm and the tops are slightly golden.

Cool and Serve:

Let the muffins cool in the pan for a few minutes before

removing. Serve warm or allow to cool completely and store for later use.

Nutritional Benefits: These egg muffins are a great source of protein and vegetables. They can be made ahead of time and stored in the refrigerator for a quick and easy breakfast option.

Banana-Oat Blender Pancakes

Nutritional Value(Per Servings): Calories: Approx 300-350 | Protein:10-12 grams | Fat: 7-9 gramsCarbohydrates: 50-55 grams | Fiber: 6-7 grams

Sugar: 10-12 grams

Cook Time: 20 minutes

Servings: 2-3 (makes about 6 pancakes)

Ingredients:

2 ripe bananas

2 cups rolled oats

1 1/2 cups milk (any kind, including dairy or plant-based)

2 eggs

1 tablespoon honey or maple syrup (optional)

1 teaspoon vanilla extract

1 1/2 teaspoons baking powder

1/2 teaspoon cinnamon

Pinch of salt

Cooking spray or a small amount of butter/oil for the pan

Instructions:

Blend the Ingredients:

Place the bananas, oats, milk, eggs, honey (if using), vanilla extract, baking powder, cinnamon, and salt in a blender. Blend on high until the mixture is smooth and the oats are fully ground.

Preheat the Pan:

Heat a non-stick skillet or griddle over medium heat. Lightly grease with cooking spray or a dab of butter or oil.

Cook the Pancakes:

Pour about 1/4 cup of batter for each pancake onto the hot skillet.

Cook for 2-3 minutes on one side, or until small bubbles form on the surface and the edges begin to look set. Flip with a spatula and cook for another 2 minutes on the other side, or until golden brown.

Serve Warm:

Serve the pancakes warm with your choice of toppings, such as fresh fruit, a drizzle of maple syrup, or a dollop of yogurt.

Nutritional Benefits: These pancakes are made with whole ingredients and are naturally sweetened with banana. They are high in fiber, vitamins, and minerals, making them a nutritious breakfast option.

Shakshuka with Feta

Nutritional Value(Per Servings): Calories: 280 kcal | Protein:15 grams | Fat: 18g

Carbohydrates: 16 grams | Fiber: 4 grams | Cholesterol: 210 mg

Sugar:8g | Sodium: 580 mg

Cook Time: 30 minutes | Total Time:40 minutes

Servings: 4

Ingredients:

Olive oil: 2 tablespoons

Onion, finely chopped: 1 medium

Garlic, minced: 2 cloves

Bell pepper, seeded and diced: 1 large

Ground cumin: 1 teaspoon

Paprika: 1 teaspoon

Cayenne pepper: 1/4 teaspoon (optional, adjust for spice level)

Canned diced tomatoes: 1 (28-ounce) can

Salt: To taste

Black pepper: To taste

Eggs: 6

Feta cheese, crumbled: 100 grams (about 1 cup)

Fresh parsley, chopped for garnish

Crusty bread or pita, for serving

Instructions:

Prepare the Vegetables:

Heat olive oil in a large skillet over medium heat. Add the chopped onion and bell pepper, and cook until the vegetables are soft, about 5 minutes. Stir in the minced garlic and cook for another minute until fragrant.

Add Spices and Tomatoes:

Sprinkle in the cumin, paprika, and cayenne pepper. Cook for a minute to release their flavors. Pour in the diced tomatoes with their juices, season with salt and pepper, and stir the mixture well.

Reduce the heat and let the sauce simmer for about 10-15 minutes, or until it thickens slightly.

Cook the Eggs:

Make wells in the tomato mixture with a spoon and crack an egg into each well. Sprinkle the crumbled feta around the eggs. Cover the skillet, and cook on low heat for about 10 minutes, or until the eggs are just set.

Garnish and Serve:

Sprinkle chopped parsley over the top. Serve hot directly from the skillet with crusty bread or warm pita to soak up the sauce.

Nutritional Benefits: This Mediterranean-inspired dish is rich in flavor and nutrients. Eggs provide protein, while tomatoes are a good source of vitamins A and C. Feta cheese adds a creamy texture and a tangy flavor.

Spinach and Feta Breakfast Quesadilla

Nutritional Value(Per Servings): Calories:350 kcal | Protein:18 grams | Fat: 20g

Carbohydrates: 27 grams | Fiber: 5 grams | Cholesterol: 210 mg

Sugar:3g | Sodium: 680 mg

Cook Time: 15 minutes | Total Time:20 minutes

Servings: 2

Ingredients:

4 whole grain tortillas

1 cup fresh spinach leaves, washed and chopped

1/2 cup crumbled feta cheese

1/2 cup diced tomatoes (optional)

2 large eggs, lightly beaten

1 small onion, finely chopped

2 cloves garlic, minced

2 tablespoons olive oil

Salt and pepper to taste

Chili flakes (optional, for added spice)

Instructions:

Preheat a skillet: Heat one tablespoon of olive oil over medium heat in a large skillet.

Sauté vegetables: Add the chopped onion and minced garlic to the skillet. Sauté until the onions become translucent, about 3-4 minutes.

Add spinach: Add the chopped spinach to the skillet and cook until just wilted, about 2 minutes. Season with salt, pepper, and chili flakes if using.

Cook eggs: Push the vegetables to one side of the skillet, and add the beaten eggs to the other side. Scramble the eggs gently as they cook. Mix them with the vegetables once fully cooked.

Assemble quesadilla: Lay out two tortillas on a clean surface. Divide the spinach and egg mixture evenly between them, spreading over half of each tortilla. Sprinkle crumbled feta cheese and diced tomatoes over the top. Fold the other half of each tortilla over to cover the filling.

Cook quesadillas: Wipe the skillet clean and heat another tablespoon of olive oil. Place the folded quesadillas in the skillet and cook on medium heat until each side is golden brown and crispy, about 2-3 minutes per side.

Serve: Cut each quesadilla into halves or quarters and serve hot.

Nutritional Benefits: This breakfast quesadilla is a great source of protein, fiber, and calcium. Spinach adds vitamins and minerals, making it a nutritious and satisfying meal

Lunch Recipes

Explore the vibrant flavors of the Atlantic coast with our collection of lunch recipes. Each dish, from hearty seafood stews to light, olive oil-dressed salads, is designed to be both nourishing and delicious. These recipes emphasize fresh, seasonal ingredients, offering a perfect balance of health and taste to re energize your afternoons.

Grilled Salmon Salad

Nutritional Value(Per Servings): Calories:450 kcal | Protein:36 grams | Fat: 28g

Carbohydrates: 15 grams | Fiber: 6 grams | Cholesterol: 85 mg

Sugar:5g | Sodium: 200 mg

Cook Time: 15 minutes | Total Time:25 minutes | Prep Time: 10 minutes

Servings: 4

Ingredients:

4 salmon fillets

Salt and freshly ground black pepper, to taste

2 tablespoons olive oil

1 tablespoon lemon juice

1 teaspoon honey

1 garlic clove, minced

8 cups mixed greens (such as arugula, spinach, and romaine)

1 cup cherry tomatoes, halved

1 avocado, peeled, pitted, and sliced

1/2 red onion, thinly sliced

1/4 cup feta cheese, crumbled (optional)

2 tablespoons capers (optional)

Lemon wedges, for serving

Dressing:

3 tablespoons olive oil

1 tablespoon white wine vinegar

1 tablespoon lemon juice

1 teaspoon Dijon mustard

1 small garlic clove, minced

Salt and pepper, to taste

Instructions:

Preheat the Grill:

Preheat your grill to medium-high heat.

Prepare the Salmon:

Season the salmon fillets with salt and pepper. In a small bowl, whisk together olive oil, lemon juice, honey, and minced garlic.

Brush this mixture over both sides of the salmon fillets.

Grill the Salmon:

Place the salmon on the grill and cook for about 6-7 minutes on each side or until the salmon is fully cooked and flakes easily with a fork.

Make the Salad Dressing:

In a small bowl, whisk together the olive oil, white wine vinegar, lemon juice, Dijon mustard, minced garlic, salt, and pepper. Adjust seasoning as needed.

Assemble the Salad:

In a large bowl, toss the mixed greens, cherry tomatoes, avocado slices, red onion, and capers (if using). Drizzle the salad with the prepared dressing and toss to combine.

Serve:

Divide the salad among plates. Top each with a grilled salmon fillet and sprinkle with feta cheese if desired. Serve with lemon wedges on the side.

Nutritional Benefits:

Salmon is rich in omega-3 fatty acids, which are beneficial for heart health.

Salad greens, cucumber, bell pepper, and red onion are high in vitamins, minerals, and antioxidants.

Olive oil is a healthy source of monounsaturated fat.

Tips:

- You can substitute grilled chicken or shrimp for the salmon if desired.

- Add cooked quinoa or brown rice for extra fiber and nutrients.

- This recipe is just one example of a lunch option that fits the Atlantic diet principles. You can include more recipes, each with its own nutritional benefits and variations.

Tuna and White Bean Salad

Nutritional Value(Per Servings): CaloriesApprox. 250 | Protein:22 grams | Fat: 9g Carbohydrates: 23 grams | Fiber: 6 gram | Sodium: Moderate

Cook Time:(no cooking required) | Total Time:15 minutes | Prep Time: 15minutes

Servings: 4

Ingredients:

2 cans (about 5 ounces each) of tuna in olive oil, drained

1 can (15 ounces) of white beans (cannellini or navy), rinsed and drained

1 medium red onion, thinly sliced

1 cup of cherry tomatoes, halved

1/2 cup of fresh parsley, chopped

2 tablespoons of capers, rinsed

Juice of 1 lemon

2 tablespoons extra virgin olive oil

Salt and pepper, to taste

Optional: a few leaves of fresh basil for garnish

Instructions:

Combine Ingredients: In a large bowl, mix the drained white beans, sliced red onion, cherry tomatoes, and capers.

Add Tuna: Flake the tuna and add it to the bowl. Gently mix to ensure the tuna remains chunky and the beans don't break apart.

Dress the Salad: Add the lemon juice and extra virgin olive oil to the salad. Toss everything gently to coat. Season with salt and pepper to taste.

Garnish and Serve: Sprinkle the chopped parsley (and basil, if using) over the top just before serving.

Nutritional Benefits:

Tuna is a good source of protein and omega-3 fatty acids.

White beans are high in fiber and protein.

Olive oil provides healthy fats and antioxidants.

Shrimp and Vegetable Stir-Fry

Nutritional Value(Per Servings): Calories: Approx. 250 | Protein: 24 grams | Fat: 12g Carbohydrates: 12 grams | Fiber: 3 gram | Sodium: 350mg

Cook Time:20 minutes | Total Time:30 minutes

Servings: 4

Ingredients:

400 grams (about 1 pound) of shrimp, peeled and deveined

2 tablespoons olive oil

1 red bell pepper, thinly sliced

1 green bell pepper, thinly sliced

1 medium onion, thinly sliced

2 cloves garlic, minced

1 zucchini, sliced into half-moons

100 grams snap peas

1 tablespoon soy sauce (or tamari for gluten-free option)

2 teaspoons sesame oil

Salt and pepper to taste

Optional: 1 teaspoon of fresh grated ginger

Optional: Sesame seeds and chopped green onions for garnish

Instructions:

Preparation:

Clean and prep all the vegetables and shrimp. Make sure the shrimp are dry to ensure they sear well in the pan.

Cook the Shrimp:

Heat 1 tablespoon of olive oil in a large skillet or wok over medium-high heat.

Add the shrimp and season with a little salt and pepper. Cook until the shrimp turn pink and are slightly golden, about 1-2 minutes per side.

Remove the shrimp from the skillet and set aside.

Sauté the Vegetables:

In the same skillet, add the remaining olive oil.

Add the onions and garlic, sautéing until the onions become translucent.

Add the bell peppers, zucchini, and snap peas. Stir-fry for about 5-7 minutes until the vegetables are just tender but still crisp.

Combine and Season:

Return the shrimp to the skillet with the vegetables.

Add soy sauce and sesame oil, and if using, the grated ginger. Stir everything together and adjust seasoning with salt and pepper.

Serve:

Serve hot, garnished with sesame seeds and chopped green onions if desired. This dish can be served over a bed of rice or noodles for a heartier meal.

Nutritional Benefits:

Shrimp is low in calories and high in protein.

Bell peppers, snow peas, and carrots are rich in vitamins and antioxidants.

Brown rice is a whole grain that provides fiber and nutrients.

Grilled Vegetable Wrap

Nutritional Value(Per Servings): Calories: Approx. 250 | Protein: 6 grams | Fat: 12g | Carbohydrates: 34 grams | Fiber: 6 gram | Sugar: 8g

Cook Time:20 minutes | Prep Time:15 minutes

Servings: 4

Ingredients:

2 zucchinis, sliced lengthwise

1 red bell pepper, deseeded and cut into wide strips

1 yellow bell pepper, deseeded and cut into wide strips

1 eggplant, sliced into rounds

1 red onion, sliced into rings

4 whole wheat tortillas

1 tablespoon olive oil

Salt and pepper, to taste

Optional: 1/4 cup hummus or Greek yogurt

Optional: fresh herbs such as parsley or cilantro, chopped

Optional: a sprinkle of feta cheese or vegan alternative

Dressing:

2 tablespoons olive oil

1 tablespoon balsamic vinegar

1 teaspoon Dijon mustard

Salt and pepper, to taste.

Instructions:

Preheat Grill: Preheat your grill to medium-high heat.

Prepare Vegetables: Brush the zucchini, bell peppers, eggplant, and onion with olive oil and season with salt and pepper.

Grill Vegetables: Place the vegetables on the grill and cook for about 3-4 minutes on each side, or until they are nicely charred and tender. Remove from the grill and set aside to cool slightly.

Prepare Dressing: In a small bowl, whisk together olive oil, balsamic vinegar, Dijon mustard, salt, and pepper.

Assemble Wraps: Spread each tortilla with a tablespoon of hummus or Greek yogurt. Arrange an even portion of grilled vegetables in the center of each tortilla. Drizzle with the dressing and sprinkle with fresh herbs and feta cheese.

Wrap and Serve: Fold the sides of the tortilla over the vegetables, then roll up tightly to enclose the filling. Cut in half and serve immediately.

Nutritional Benefits:

Grilled vegetables are low in calories and rich in vitamins and antioxidants.

Whole grain wraps provide fiber and nutrients.

Hummus adds protein and healthy fats.

Smoked Salmon and Avocado Sandwich

Nutritional Value(Per Servings): Calories: 400 kcal | Protein: 21grams | Fat: 20g| Carbohydrates: 33 grams | Fiber: 7 gram

Cook Time:0 minutes | Prep Time:10 minutes | Total Time: 10 minutes

Servings: 2

Ingredients:

4 slices of whole grain bread

4 oz smoked salmon

1 ripe avocado, sliced

2 tablespoons cream cheese (optional, can use a low-fat or dairy-free version)

1 tablespoon lemon juice

1 small red onion, thinly sliced

Fresh dill, chopped (to taste)

Salt and pepper, to taste

Optional: capers for garnish

Instructions:

Prepare the Bread: Toast the whole grain bread slices until they are nicely browned and crispy. This adds texture and flavor to the sandwich.

Mix Cream Cheese (Optional): If using cream cheese, mix it with the lemon juice and a pinch of salt. Spread it evenly over two slices of the toasted bread. This step is optional; you can skip the cream cheese for a lighter version.

Assemble the Sandwich: Lay the smoked salmon slices evenly over the bread with the cream cheese.

Add the sliced avocado on top of the salmon. Avocado adds creaminess and a rich, buttery texture that complements the smoky flavor of the salmon.

Sprinkle with chopped dill, salt, and pepper to taste. The dill enhances the fish with its fresh, slightly anise-like flavor.

Add the sliced red onion for a sharp, crunchy contrast.

If desired, add a few capers for an extra burst of tangy flavor.

Final Touches: Cover with the remaining slices of bread. Press down gently to ensure the sandwich holds together well.

Serve: Cut the sandwich in half and serve immediately for the best taste and texture.

Nutritional Benefits:

Smoked salmon is rich in omega-3 fatty acids.

Avocado provides healthy fats and fiber.

Whole grain bread is a good source of fiber and nutrients.

Lentil and Vegetable Soup

Nutritional Value(Per Servings): Calories: 250kcal | Protein: 14 grams | Fat: 7g|

Carbohydrates: 37grams | Fiber: 9 grams

Cook Time:45 minutes | Prep Time:15 minutes

Servings: 4

Ingredients:

1 cup dried green lentils, rinsed

2 tablespoons olive oil

1 large onion, chopped

2 garlic cloves, minced

2 carrots, peeled and diced

2 stalks celery, diced

1 small zucchini, diced

1 red bell pepper, diced

1 teaspoon dried thyme

1 teaspoon dried rosemary

1 bay leaf

4 cups vegetable broth

2 cups water

1 can (14 oz) diced tomatoes, with juice

Salt and pepper, to taste

Fresh parsley, chopped (for garnish)

Instructions:

Prepare the Lentils: In a medium saucepan, bring lentils and enough water to cover by a few inches to a boil. Reduce heat and simmer for about 20 minutes, or until lentils are tender. Drain and set aside.

Sauté Vegetables: In a large pot, heat olive oil over medium heat. Add onion and garlic, sautéing until onion is translucent. Add carrots, celery, zucchini, and bell pepper, cooking until they start to soften, about 5 minutes.

Add Herbs and Liquids: Stir in thyme, rosemary, and bay leaf. Pour in vegetable broth, water, and diced tomatoes with their juice. Bring to a simmer.

Combine Lentils: Add cooked lentils to the pot. Season with salt and pepper. Simmer the soup for another 15 minutes, allowing flavors to meld.

Final Touches: Remove bay leaf. Adjust seasoning as needed. Serve hot, garnished with fresh parsley.

Nutritional Benefits:

Lentils are high in protein and fiber.

Vegetables provide vitamins, minerals, and antioxidants.

Vegetable broth adds flavor without extra calories.

Quinoa and Black Bean Salad

Nutritional Value(Per Servings): Calories: 330 | Protein: 10 grams | Fat: 15g

Carbohydrates: 42grams | Fiber: 9 grams

Cook Time:25 minutes

Servings: 4

Ingredients:

1 cup quinoa

2 cups water

1 can (15 oz) black beans, drained and rinsed

1 medium red bell pepper, diced

1/4 cup finely chopped red onion

1/4 cup chopped fresh cilantro

Juice of 2 limes

3 tablespoons olive oil

Salt and pepper to taste

1 avocado, diced

1/2 cup corn kernels (optional)

Instructions:

Rinse quinoa under cold water. In a medium saucepan, bring 2 cups of water to a boil. Add quinoa, reduce heat to low, cover, and simmer for 15 minutes or until water is absorbed. Remove from heat and let sit covered for 5 minutes.

Fluff the cooked quinoa with a fork and allow it to cool.

In a large bowl, combine cooled quinoa, black beans, bell pepper, onion, cilantro, and corn if using.

In a small bowl, whisk together lime juice, olive oil, salt, and pepper. Pour over the quinoa mixture and toss to coat evenly.

Gently fold in diced avocado.

Serve chilled or at room temperature.

Nutritional Benefits:

Quinoa is a complete protein and a good source of fiber.

Black beans are high in protein and fiber.

Bell peppers and red onion provide vitamins and antioxidants.

Baked Cod with Roasted Vegetables

Nutritional Value(Per Servings): Calories: 280 | Protein: 35 grams | Fat: 9g

Carbohydrates: 15 grams | Fiber: 4 grams

Cook Time: 40 minutes

Servings: 4

Ingredients:

4 cod fillets (6 oz each)

2 tablespoons olive oil

Salt and pepper to taste

1 teaspoon paprika

2 zucchinis, sliced

2 bell peppers, assorted colors, sliced

1 small red onion, sliced

2 cloves garlic, minced

Lemon wedges, for serving

Instructions:

Preheat oven to 400°F (200°C).

Place the cod fillets on a greased baking sheet. Brush each fillet with olive oil and season with salt, pepper, and paprika.

In a large bowl, toss the zucchini, bell peppers, onion,

and garlic with olive oil and season with salt and pepper.

Spread the vegetables around the cod on the baking sheet.

Bake in the preheated oven for 25-30 minutes, until the vegetables are caramelized and the cod flakes easily with a fork.

Serve hot with lemon wedges.

Nutritional Benefits:

Cod is a lean source of protein and is rich in vitamins and minerals.

Zucchini, yellow squash, bell peppers, and red onion are low in calories and high in vitamins and antioxidants.

Olive oil provides healthy fats and adds flavor to the dish.

Chickpea and Spinach Stew

Nutritional Value(Per Servings): Calories: 220 | Protein: 10 grams | Fat: 6g

Carbohydrates: 33 grams | Fiber: 9 grams | Sugar: 7g

Cook Time: 30 minutes

Servings: 4

Ingredients:

1 tablespoon olive oil

1 onion, chopped

2 cloves garlic, minced

1 teaspoon ground cumin

1/2 teaspoon smoked paprika

1 can (15 oz) chickpeas, drained and rinsed

1 can (14.5 oz) diced tomatoes

4 cups fresh spinach

Salt and pepper to taste

1/4 cup plain Greek yogurt (optional, for serving)

Instructions:

Heat olive oil in a large pot over medium heat. Add onion and garlic, sautéing until onion is translucent.

Stir in cumin and smoked paprika, cook for another minute until fragrant.

Add chickpeas and tomatoes. Bring to a simmer and cook for 20 minutes.

Stir in spinach and cook until wilted, about 3 minutes. Season with salt and pepper.

Serve hot, topped with a dollop of Greek yogurt if desired.

Nutritional Benefits:

Chickpeas are high in protein and fiber.

Spinach is a good source of vitamins and minerals.

Tomatoes provide lycopene, a powerful antioxidant.

Turkey and Avocado Wrap

Nutritional Value(Per Servings): Calories: 350 | Protein: 21 grams | Fat: 18g

Carbohydrates: 27 grams | Fiber: 5 grams | Sugar: 3g

Cook Time:10 minutes

Servings: 4

Ingredients:

4 whole wheat wraps

8 slices turkey breast

1 ripe avocado, sliced

1/4 cup mayonnaise or Greek yogurt

1 cup mixed salad greens

1 tomato, sliced

Salt and pepper to taste

Instructions:

Spread each wrap with a thin layer of mayonnaise or Greek yogurt.

Layer turkey slices, avocado slices, salad greens, and tomato slices on each wrap. Season with salt and pepper.

Roll up the wraps tightly and cut in half.

Serve immediately or wrap in foil for a grab-and-go lunch.

Nutritional Benefits:

Turkey is a lean source of protein.

Avocado provides healthy fats and fiber.

Greek yogurt adds protein and creaminess to the wrap.

Dinner Recipes

Dinner is a time to unwind and indulge in the rich culinary traditions of the Atlantic coast. This section offers a collection of dishes that embody the essence of the Atlantic Diet, featuring fresh seafood, vibrant vegetables, and hearty grains. Each recipe is designed to deliver not only nourishment but also the comfort of wholesome, home-cooked meals. From quick weeknight dinners to impressive dishes for special occasions, these recipes celebrate the natural abundance and flavors of the Atlantic regions. Enjoy crafting these meals that are sure to bring warmth and satisfaction to your dinner table.

Grilled Salmon with Lemon and Dill

Nutritional Value(Per Servings): Calories: 290 | Protein: 23 grams | Fat: 22g

Carbohydrates: 1 grams | Omega-3 Fatty Acids: ~2g

Cook Time: 20 minutes

Servings: 4

Ingredients:

4 salmon fillets (6 oz each)

2 tablespoons olive oil

Juice of 1 lemon

1 tablespoon fresh dill, chopped

Salt and pepper to taste

Lemon slices and additional dill for garnish

Instructions:

Preheat your grill to medium-high heat.

In a small bowl, mix together olive oil, lemon juice, chopped dill, salt, and pepper.

Brush each salmon fillet with the olive oil mixture.

Place the salmon on the grill, skin-side down, and cover. Cook for about 6-8 minutes on each side or until the salmon is cooked through and flakes easily with a fork. Remove from the grill and garnish with lemon slices and additional dill.

Nutritional Benefits: Salmon is rich in omega-3 fatty acids, which are beneficial for heart health. It is also a good source of protein and vitamin D.

Atlantic Fish Stew

Nutritional Value(Per Servings): Calories: 350 | Protein: 28 grams | Fat: 18g

Carbohydrates: 15 grams | Fiber: 3 grams | Sugar: 6g | Cholesterol: 85 mg |

Sodium: 800 mg

Cook Time: 30 minutes Prep Time: 15 minutes

Total Time: 45 minutes

Servings: 4

Ingredients:

2 tablespoons olive oil

1 large onion, finely chopped

2 garlic cloves, minced

1 bell pepper, diced

2 medium carrots, sliced

1 teaspoon smoked paprika

1/4 teaspoon saffron threads (optional)

400g canned diced tomatoes

1 liter fish or vegetable stock

500g mixed fresh seafood (e.g., chunks of white fish, prawns, mussels)

200g firm white fish, cut into chunks

100g chorizo, sliced (optional)

Salt and pepper, to taste

Fresh parsley, chopped, for garnish

Lemon wedges, for serving

Instructions:

Heat the Oil:

In a large pot, heat the olive oil over medium heat. Add the onion and garlic and sauté until the onion is translucent, about 5 minutes.

Add Vegetables and Spices:

Add the bell pepper and carrots to the pot, cooking for another 5 minutes until slightly softened. Stir in the smoked paprika and saffron threads, cooking for 1 minute until fragrant.

Simmer the Base:

Pour in the diced tomatoes and stock, bringing the mixture to a boil. Reduce the heat to a simmer, cover, and let cook for about 15 minutes.

Add Seafood:

Add the mixed seafood, white fish chunks, and chorizo (if using) to the pot. Season with salt and pepper. Cover and simmer for another 10 minutes, or until the seafood is cooked through and the flavors are well combined.

Garnish and Serve:

Check the seasoning and adjust if necessary. Garnish with fresh parsley and serve with lemon wedges on the side.

Nutritional Benefits: This stew is packed with protein from the fish and shrimp, as well as vitamins and minerals from the vegetables. The broth provides a flavorful base without added fats.

Atlantic Diet Shrimp and Vegetable Stir-Fry

Nutritional Value(Per Servings): Calories: Approx 250| Protein: 24 grams | Fat: 10g Carbohydrates: 15 grams | Fiber: 3 grams | Sugar: 6g | Sodium:Moderate

Cook Time:15 minutes Prep Time: 10 minutes

Total Time: 25 minutes

Servings: 4

Ingredients:

450 grams (1 pound) of shrimp, peeled and deveined

2 tablespoons of olive oil

1 red bell pepper, sliced

1 yellow bell pepper, sliced

1 medium zucchini, sliced

1 medium onion, sliced

2 cloves of garlic, minced

200 grams (about 1 cup) of snap peas

1 tablespoon of low-sodium soy sauce (or tamari for a gluten-free option)

1 tablespoon of oyster sauce (optional)

Juice of 1 lemon

Salt and pepper, to taste

Fresh parsley or cilantro, chopped (for garnish)

Optional: chili flakes or fresh chili for a bit of heat

Instructions:

Prepare Ingredients:

Clean and chop all the vegetables as described. Peel and devein the shrimp if not already prepared.

Heat the Pan:

Heat the olive oil in a large skillet or wok over medium-high heat.

Sauté Vegetables:

Add the onions and garlic to the pan and sauté for about 2 minutes until the onions begin to soften.

Add the bell peppers, zucchini, and snap peas. Stir-fry for about 5 minutes until just tender but still crisp.

Cook the Shrimp:

Add the shrimp to the pan, stirring frequently. Cook for about 3-4 minutes or until the shrimp are pink and opaque.

Season the Dish:

Add the soy sauce, oyster sauce (if using), and lemon juice. Stir well to combine all ingredients. Season with salt, pepper, and chili flakes (if using). Cook for an additional minute to blend the flavors.

Garnish and Serve:

Remove from heat and garnish with fresh parsley or cilantro. Serve immediately.

Nutritional Benefits: This stir-fry is high in protein from the shrimp and packed with vitamins and minerals from the vegetables. The soy sauce adds flavor without a lot of extra calories.

Cod with Tomato and Olive Sauce

Nutritional Value(Per Servings): Calories: Approx 250 | Protein: 27 grams | Fat: 10g Carbohydrates: 10 grams | Fiber: 2 grams | Sodium:300mg

Cook Time:30 minutes Prep Time: 10 minutes

Total Time: 40 minutes

Servings: 4

Ingredients:

4 cod fillets (about 6 ounces each)

2 tablespoons olive oil

1 medium onion, finely chopped

3 cloves garlic, minced

1 red bell pepper, diced

1 can (14 oz) diced tomatoes

1/2 cup pitted black olives, sliced

1/4 cup fresh parsley, chopped

1 tablespoon capers (optional)

Salt and pepper, to taste

Lemon wedges, for serving

Instructions:

Prepare the Ingredients:

Pat the cod fillets dry with paper towels and season both sides with salt and pepper. Prepare the onion, garlic, and bell pepper as noted.

Cook the Vegetables:

Heat the olive oil in a large skillet over medium heat.

Add the chopped onion and bell pepper. Cook for about 5 minutes or until the vegetables start to soften.

Add the minced garlic and cook for another minute until fragrant.

Simmer the Tomato Sauce:

Stir in the diced tomatoes with their juice, olives, and capers (if using). Bring to a simmer. Let the sauce simmer gently for about 10 minutes to blend the flavors, stirring occasionally.

Cook the Cod:

Nestle the cod fillets into the sauce in the skillet. Cover and cook over medium-low heat for about 10-12 minutes, or until the cod is opaque and flakes easily with a fork.

Finish and Serve:

Sprinkle the chopped parsley over the dish just before serving.

Serve the cod with a side of the tomato and olive sauce, garnished with lemon wedges.

Nutritional Benefits: Cod is a lean source of protein that is rich in vitamins B12 and B6, as well as selenium and phosphorus. Tomatoes and olives add antioxidants and healthy fats to the dish.

Atlantic Diet Clam and Vegetable Pasta

Nutritional Value(Per Servings): Calories: Approx 450 | Protein: 22 grams | Fat: 10g Carbohydrates: 72 grams | Fiber: 8 grams

Cook Time:20 minutes Prep Time: 20 minutes

Total Time: 40 minutes

Servings: 4

Ingredients:

400 grams (14 oz) whole grain pasta (such as spaghetti or linguine)

2 tablespoons extra virgin olive oil

4 garlic cloves, minced

1 small red onion, thinly sliced

1 red bell pepper, thinly sliced

1 zucchini, sliced into half-moons

1 carrot, julienned

400 grams (14 oz) canned clams, drained, reserve the juice

200 grams (7 oz) cherry tomatoes, halved

1 teaspoon crushed red pepper flakes (optional)

Salt and freshly ground black pepper, to taste

Fresh parsley, chopped (for garnish)

Grated lemon zest (for garnish)

Instructions:

Prepare the Pasta:

Bring a large pot of salted water to a boil. Add the pasta and cook according to the package instructions until al dente. Drain and set aside, reserving 1 cup of the pasta cooking water.

Cook the Vegetables:

While the pasta is cooking, heat the olive oil in a large skillet over medium heat. Add the garlic and onion, sautéing until the onion becomes translucent, about 3-5 minutes.

Add the bell pepper, zucchini, and carrot. Cook, stirring occasionally, until the vegetables are tender, about 5-7 minutes.

Add Clams and Tomatoes:

Stir in the clams, cherry tomatoes, and red pepper flakes if using. Cook until the tomatoes start to break down, about 3-4 minutes.

Pour in the reserved clam juice and a splash of the reserved pasta water to create a light sauce. Let simmer for another 2-3 minutes. Adjust seasoning with salt and black pepper.

Combine Pasta and Serve:

Add the cooked pasta to the skillet and toss everything together until the pasta is well coated with the sauce and heated through. If the pasta seems dry, add a bit more of the reserved pasta water.

Serve hot, garnished with fresh parsley and grated lemon zest.

Nutritional Benefits: This pasta dish is high in fiber from the whole grain pasta and vegetables. Clams are a good source of protein and iron, while olive oil adds heart-healthy monounsaturated fats.

Atlantic Diet Baked Stuffed Peppers

Nutritional Value(Per Servings): Calories: Approx 350 | Protein: 26 grams | Fat: 15g Carbohydrates: 35 grams | Fiber: 5 grams | Sugar: 8g

Cook Time:45 minutes Prep Time: 20 minutes

Total Time: 65 minutes

Servings: 4

Ingredients:

4 large bell peppers, any color

1 tablespoon olive oil

1 onion, finely chopped

2 cloves garlic, minced

1 cup whole grain rice or quinoa, cooked

300 grams ground turkey or a mix of seafood (like chopped shrimp and crab)

1 cup chopped tomatoes

1/2 cup chopped parsley

1 teaspoon smoked paprika

Salt and pepper, to taste

1/4 cup crumbled feta or goat cheese (optional)

Fresh lemon juice (for drizzling)

Instructions:

Prepare the Peppers:

Preheat your oven to 375°F (190°C).

Slice the tops off the peppers and remove the seeds and membranes. If necessary, slightly trim the bottoms to help them stand upright in the baking dish without cutting into the cavity.

Cook the Filling:

Heat the olive oil in a skillet over medium heat. Add the chopped onion and garlic, sautéing until translucent.

Add the ground turkey or seafood, cooking until browned and cooked through.

Mix in the cooked rice or quinoa, chopped tomatoes, parsley, and smoked paprika. Season with salt and pepper. Cook together for another 5 minutes until everything is well combined.

Stuff the Peppers:

Spoon the filling into the hollowed-out peppers, packing it tightly.

Top each pepper with crumbled cheese if using.

Bake:

Place the stuffed peppers in a baking dish. Cover loosely with foil to prevent burning.

Bake in the preheated oven for about 30-35 minutes, or until the peppers are tender and the filling is hot.

Serve:

Remove from oven, drizzle with fresh lemon juice, and serve warm.

Nutritional Benefits: This dish is a complete meal, providing protein from the quinoa and black beans, fiber from the vegetables, and a variety of vitamins and minerals. The colors of the peppers indicate the different antioxidants they contain.

Atlantic Diet Seafood Paella

Nutritional Value(Per Servings): Calories: Approx 350-400 kcal | Protein: 25 grams | Fat: 10g Carbohydrates: 55 grams | Fiber: 4 grams

Cook Time:50 minutes Total Time: 1 hour 10 minutes

Servings: 4-6

Ingredients:

- 1 tablespoon olive oil
- 1 onion, finely chopped
- 2 cloves garlic, minced
- 1 red bell pepper, sliced
- 1 yellow bell pepper, sliced
- 250 grams (about 1/2 pound) tomatoes, chopped
- 1 teaspoon smoked paprika
- 1/2 teaspoon saffron threads
- 1 cup short-grain rice, such as Bomba or Arborio
- 500 ml (about 2 cups) fish or vegetable stock
- 300 grams (about 2/3 pound) mixed seafood (e.g., shrimp, mussels, and squid rings)
- 150 grams (about 1/3 pound) firm white fish, such as cod or halibut, cubed
- 1/2 cup peas (fresh or frozen)
- Salt and pepper, to taste
- Lemon wedges, for serving

Fresh parsley, chopped, for garnish

Instructions:

Prepare Ingredients:

Heat the olive oil in a large skillet or paella pan over medium heat.

Add the onion and garlic, sautéing until the onion is translucent.

Mix in the red and yellow bell peppers and cook until they start to soften.

Cook Rice with Seasonings:

Stir in the chopped tomatoes, smoked paprika, and saffron threads, cooking until the tomatoes break down.

Add the rice, stirring to coat it in the mixture, then pour in the stock. Bring to a simmer.

Simmer Paella:

Reduce the heat to low and let the rice cook, uncovered, for about 20 minutes, or until it's halfway done. Do not stir; this allows the bottom of the rice to caramelize slightly.

Add Seafood:

Nestle the mixed seafood and cubed fish into the partially cooked rice. Sprinkle the peas over the top.

Continue to cook without stirring, allowing the rice to absorb the liquid and the seafood to cook, about 10-15 more minutes.

Check and Garnish:

Check the rice and seafood for doneness. Adjust the seasoning with salt and pepper.

Remove from heat and let it sit for a few minutes. Serve with lemon wedges and garnish with fresh parsley.

Nutritional Benefits: This paella is a complete meal, providing protein from the seafood, fiber from the brown rice and vegetables, and a variety of vitamins and minerals. Saffron adds a unique flavor and color to the dish.

Atlantic Diet Baked Cod with Potatoes and Olives

Nutritional Value(Per Servings): Calories: Approx 350 kcal | Protein: 27 grams | Fat: 12g Carbohydrates: 34 grams | Fiber: 5 grams | Sodium: 300mg

Cook Time:45 minutes Prep Time: 15 minute Total Time: 1 hour

Servings: 4

Ingredients:

4 cod fillets (about 6 ounces each)

4 medium potatoes, thinly sliced

1/2 cup black olives, pitted and halved

2 tomatoes, sliced

1 onion, thinly sliced

3 cloves garlic, minced

1 lemon, sliced

2 tablespoons olive oil

Fresh parsley, chopped (for garnish)

Salt and pepper to taste

Instructions:

Preheat the Oven: Preheat your oven to 400°F (200°C).

Prepare the Vegetables: Arrange the sliced potatoes, onions, and tomatoes in a large baking dish. Drizzle with one tablespoon of olive oil and sprinkle with salt and pepper. Toss everything to coat evenly.

Bake the Vegetables: Place the baking dish in the preheated oven and bake for about 20 minutes, or until the potatoes start to become tender.

Prepare the Cod: While the vegetables are baking, season the cod fillets with salt, pepper, and minced garlic.

Add Cod and Olives to the Dish: Remove the baking dish from the oven. Place the cod fillets on top of the semi-cooked vegetables. Scatter the black olives and lemon slices around the cod.

Bake Again: Drizzle the remaining tablespoon of olive oil over the cod and vegetables. Return the dish to the oven and bake for an additional 20-25 minutes, or until the cod is flaky and the potatoes are fully tender.

Garnish and Serve: Remove from the oven and garnish with fresh chopped parsley before serving.

Nutritional Benefits: This dish is rich in protein from the cod, and the potatoes provide complex carbohydrates for energy. Olives add healthy fats and a unique flavor.

Atlantic Diet Roasted Vegetable Salad

Nutritional Value(Per Servings): Calories: Approx 250 kcal | Protein: 4 grams | Fat: 18g Carbohydrates: 20 grams | Fiber: 6 grams | Sodium: 300mg | Sugar: 10g

Cook Time:30 minutes Prep Time: 15 minute Total Time: 45 minutes

Servings: 4

Ingredients:

1 medium zucchini, cut into bite-sized pieces

1 red bell pepper, cut into bite-sized pieces

1 yellow bell pepper, cut into bite-sized pieces

1 small eggplant, cut into bite-sized pieces

1 red onion, sliced

2 tablespoons olive oil

Salt and freshly ground black pepper, to taste

1 cup cherry tomatoes, halved

1/4 cup pitted Kalamata olives, halved

1/4 cup feta cheese, crumbled

2 tablespoons fresh basil, chopped

2 tablespoons fresh parsley, chopped

For the Dressing:

3 tablespoons olive oil

1 tablespoon balsamic vinegar

1 teaspoon Dijon mustard

1 garlic clove, minced

Salt and pepper, to taste

Instructions:

Preheat the Oven: Preheat your oven to 425°F (220°C).

Prepare the Vegetables: In a large bowl, toss the zucchini, bell peppers, eggplant, and red onion with 2 tablespoons of olive oil, salt, and pepper. Spread the vegetables on a baking sheet in a single layer.

Roast the Vegetables: Roast in the preheated oven for about 25-30 minutes, stirring once halfway through, until the vegetables are tender and have begun to brown.

Prepare the Dressing: While the vegetables are roasting, whisk together the olive oil, balsamic vinegar, Dijon mustard, minced garlic, salt, and pepper in a small bowl. Set aside.

Assemble the Salad: Transfer the roasted vegetables to a serving bowl. Add the cherry tomatoes, olives, and crumbled feta cheese. Drizzle with the dressing and gently toss to combine.

Garnish and Serve: Sprinkle with chopped basil and parsley before serving.

Nutritional Benefits: This salad is packed with vitamins and minerals from the vegetables, and the feta cheese adds protein and calcium. The balsamic glaze adds a tangy flavor without a lot of extra calories.

Atlantic Diet Portuguese-style Chicken

Nutritional Value(Per Servings): Calories: Approx 350 kcal | Protein: 28 grams | Fat: 20g Carbohydrates: 12 grams | Fiber: 3 grams | Sodium: 320mg | Sugar: 6g

Cook Time:45 minutes Prep Time: 15 minute Total Time: 1 hour

Servings: 4

Ingredients:

4 bone-in, skin-on chicken thighs

2 tablespoons olive oil

4 cloves garlic, minced

1 large onion, sliced

1 red bell pepper, sliced

1 yellow bell pepper, sliced

2 medium tomatoes, chopped

1 teaspoon smoked paprika

1/2 teaspoon cayenne pepper (optional, adjust to taste)

1/2 cup white wine

1/2 cup chicken broth

1 lemon, juiced and zest

2 tablespoons fresh parsley, chopped

1 tablespoon fresh oregano, chopped

Salt and pepper, to taste

Instructions:

Preheat the Oven: Preheat your oven to 375°F (190°C).

Season the Chicken: Season the chicken thighs with salt, pepper, smoked paprika, and cayenne pepper.

Brown the Chicken: In a large oven-proof skillet or Dutch oven, heat the olive oil over medium-high heat. Add the chicken, skin-side down, and sear until the skin is golden and crispy, about 5-7 minutes. Flip the chicken and cook for another 3-4 minutes.

Remove the chicken and set aside.

Sauté the Vegetables: In the same skillet, add the onion and garlic, sautéing until the onion becomes translucent. Add the bell peppers and cook until they start to soften.

Deglaze and Simmer: Pour in the white wine, scraping any browned bits off the bottom of the pan. Allow the wine to reduce by half, then add the chopped tomatoes and chicken broth.

Bake: Return the chicken to the skillet, spooning some of the sauce over the top. Transfer the skillet to the oven and bake uncovered for 30 minutes, or until the chicken is fully cooked and the vegetables are tender.

Finish with Lemon and Herbs: Remove from the oven and stir in the lemon juice, zest, and fresh herbs.

Serve: Serve the chicken with a side of roasted potatoes or a fresh salad to keep it light and diet-friendly.

Nutritional Benefits: This dish is high in protein from the chicken breasts and packed with vitamins and minerals from the vegetables. The white wine adds flavor without a lot of extra calories.

Snack Recipes

Welcome to the delightful world of snack recipes! Whether you're looking for something to tide you over between meals, need a quick energy boost, or just want a tasty treat that doesn't compromise on health, this section has you covered. Our selection of snack recipes is designed to be nutritious, delicious, and easy to prepare. From fresh apple slices paired with creamy almond butter to crunchy homemade granola bars, each recipe is perfect for on-the-go moments, relaxed afternoons, or as a healthful addition to your meal plan. Let's dive into these simple yet satisfying recipes that will keep your energy levels up and your taste buds happy, without any fuss.

Smoked Salmon Cucumber Bites

Nutritional Value(Per bites): Calories: Approx 30 kcal | Protein: 2 grams | Fat: 2g Carbohydrates: 1 grams | Fiber: 0.2 grams | Sodium: 120mg | Sugar: 0.5g

Servings: 24 bites

Ingredients:

1 cucumber, sliced into rounds

100g smoked salmon, cut into small pieces

50g cream cheese

Fresh dill, for garnish

Instructions:

Spread a thin layer of cream cheese on each cucumber round.

Top with a piece of smoked salmon.

Garnish with fresh dill.

This recipe for Smoked Salmon Cucumber Bites is quick and easy, requiring no cooking and minimal prep time. It's a delightful, low-calorie snack that offers a good balance of protein and freshness, fitting perfectly within the Atlantic Diet framework. The combination of fresh cucumber with the rich flavor of smoked salmon makes for a refreshing and satisfying treat.

Olive Tapenade

Nutritional Value(Per bites): Calories: Approx 150 kcal | Protein: 1 grams | Fat: 2g Carbohydrates:4 grams | Fiber: 1 grams | Sodium: High

Servings:4-6

Ingredients:

200g black olives, pitted

2 cloves garlic, minced

2 tbsp capers

2 tbsp fresh parsley, chopped

2 tbsp lemon juice

3 tbsp olive oil

Instructions:

Place all ingredients in a food processor and blend until smooth.

Serve with whole grain crackers or sliced vegetables.

This olive tapenade is not only a delicious and versatile snack but also aligns well with the healthy, Mediterranean-inspired elements of the Atlantic Diet. Its preparation is quick and easy, making it perfect for impromptu gatherings or as a sophisticated addition to a meal.

Tuna Stuffed Avocado

Nutritional Value(Per bites): Calories: Approx 300 kcal | Protein: 18 grams | Fat: 23g Carbohydrates:9 grams | Fiber: 7 grams | Sodium: Varies based on added salt and capers/pickles

Servings:2

Ingredients:

2 avocados, halved and pitted

1 can tuna, drained

2 tbsp Greek yogurt

1 tbsp lemon juice

Salt and pepper, to taste

Instructions:

In a bowl, mix tuna, Greek yogurt, lemon juice, salt, and pepper.

Spoon the tuna mixture into the avocado halves.

Serve as is or sprinkle with paprika for extra flavor.

This recipe is rich in omega-3 fatty acids from the tuna and monounsaturated fats from the avocado, making it heart-healthy and filling. It also provides a good amount of fiber, which aids in digestion. Tuna Stuffed Avocado is perfect for a nutritious snack, a light lunch, or even as a side dish. The combination of fresh, creamy, and zesty flavors makes this a delightful addition to your healthy eating repertoire.

Baked Sweet Potato Chips

Nutritional Value(Per bites): Calories: Approx 150 kcal | Protein: 2 grams | Fat: 5g | Carbohydrates:24 grams | Fiber: 4 grams | Sodium: Variable (depends on added salt and seasonings)

Prep Time: 10 minutes | Cook Time: 25 minutes | Total Time: 35 minutes

Servings:4

Ingredients:

2 Sweet potatoes, thinly sliced

2 Tbsp olive oil

Salt and pepper, to taste

Instructions:

Preheat oven to 200°C (400°F) and line a baking sheet with parchment paper.

Toss sweet potato slices with olive oil, salt, and pepper.

Spread the sweet potato slices in a single layer on the baking sheet.

Bake for 15-20 minutes, or until crispy.

Greek Yogurt with Honey and Almonds

Nutritional Value(Per bites): Calories: Approx 350 kcal | Protein: 20 grams | Fat: 15g | Carbohydrates:35 grams | Fiber: 3 grams | Sodium: 60mg

Servings:1

Ingredients:

1 cup Greek yogurt

2 tbsp honey

2 tbsp almonds, chopped

Instructions:

Spoon Greek yogurt into a bowl.

Drizzle with honey and sprinkle with chopped almonds.

This snack is an excellent source of protein and calcium from Greek yogurt, healthy fats from almonds, and a natural sweet touch from honey. It's ideal for a quick breakfast, a mid-morning snack, or a post-workout refuel.

Roasted Red Pepper Hummus

Nutritional Value(Per bites): Calories: Approx 140 kcal | Protein: 4 grams | Fat: 8g | Carbohydrates:13 grams | Fiber: 3 grams | Sugar: 2g

Servings:6

Ingredients:

1 can (15 oz) chickpeas, drained and rinsed

1 large roasted red pepper

2 cloves garlic, minced

3 tbsp tahini

2 tbsp lemon juice

2 tbsp olive oil

Salt and pepper, to taste

Instructions:

In a food processor, combine chickpeas, roasted red pepper, garlic, tahini, lemon juice, olive oil, salt, and pepper.

Blend until smooth.

Serve with vegetable sticks or whole grain pita bread.

This Roasted Red Pepper Hummus is not only a delicious and easy-to-make snack but also offers a healthy option rich in fiber and protein, perfect for any time of the day.

Grilled Zucchini Roll-Ups

Nutritional Value(Per bites): Calories: Approx 50-70 kcal | Protein: 2-3 grams | Fat: 4-6g | Carbohydrates:3-4 grams | Fiber: 1 grams | Sugar: 2g

Servings:4-6(Makes about 12 roll-up)

Ingredients:

1 large zucchini, sliced lengthwise into thin strips

100g feta cheese, crumbled

50g sun-dried tomatoes, chopped

Fresh basil leaves

Olive oil, for grilling

Instructions:

Heat a grill pan over medium-high heat.

Brush zucchini strips with olive oil and grill for 1-2 minutes per side, until tender.

Remove from heat and let cool slightly.

Spread each zucchini strip with feta cheese and top with

sun-dried tomatoes and basil leaves.

Roll up and secure with a toothpick.

Mediterranean Chickpea Salad

Nutritional Value(Per bites): Calories: Approx 220 kcal | Protein: 7 grams | Fat: 14g | Carbohydrates:20 grams | Fiber: 5 grams | Sugar: 5g

Servings:4

Ingredients:

1 can (15 oz) chickpeas

1 cucumber, diced

1 tomato, diced

1/4 red onion, thinly sliced

2 tbsp fresh parsley, chopped

2 tbsp olive oil

1 tbsp lemon juice

Salt and pepper, to taste

Instructions:

In a large bowl, combine chickpeas, cucumber, tomato, red onion, and parsley.

Drizzle with olive oil and lemon juice.

Season with salt and pepper, and toss to combine.

This Mediterranean Chickpea Salad is not only nutritious and filling but also vibrant and bursting with flavors, making it a perfect snack or addition to any meal. Enjoy its freshness and the health benefits it brings!

Sardine Pate

Nutritional Value(Per bites): Calories: Approx 150 kcal | Protein: 13 grams | Fat: 10g | Carbohydrates:2 grams | Fiber: 0.5 grams | Sugar: 1g

Servings:4

Ingredients:

1 can (4 oz) sardines, drained

2 tbsp Greek yogurt

1 tbsp lemon juice

1 tbsp capers

1/2 tsp Dijon mustard

Salt and pepper, to taste

Instructions:

In a bowl, mash sardines with a fork.

Add Greek yogurt, lemon juice, capers, Dijon mustard, salt, and pepper. Mix until well combined.

Serve on whole grain crackers or cucumber slices.

This Sardine Paté is an excellent source of omega-3 fatty acids and protein, making it a heart-healthy choice that's also filling. Its robust flavor and creamy texture make it a popular choice for appetizers or a quick snack during the day. Enjoy this simple, flavorful preparation as a delightful part of your snack repertoire!

Apple Slices with Almond Butter

Nutritional Value(Per bites): Calories: Approx 280 kcal | Protein: 8 grams | Fat: 18g | Carbohydrates:28 grams | Fiber: 6 grams | Sugar: 18g

Servings:2

Ingredients:

1 apple, sliced

2 tbsp almond butter

Instructions:

Spread almond butter on apple slices.

Enjoy as a simple and nutritious snack.

This snack is perfect for a quick energy boost during the day or as a post-workout treat, providing a good source of dietary fiber and protein. It's also incredibly versatile and kid-friendly, making it a great addition to lunchboxes or as an after-school snack.

CHAPTER 5

Cooking Techniques for the Atlantic Diet

Cooking plays a crucial role in the Atlantic diet, emphasizing fresh ingredients and simple preparations to preserve flavors and nutrients. This section explores essential cooking techniques and tips for mastering the art of Atlantic cuisine.

Tips for Healthy Cooking

1. Grilling and Roasting

Grilling and roasting are popular cooking methods in the Atlantic diet, imparting a delicious smoky flavor to meats, fish, and vegetables. Use a grill or oven to cook foods at high temperatures, enhancing their natural flavors without the need for excess fats or oils.

Tip: Marinate meats and vegetables in herbs, spices, and citrus juices before grilling or roasting to add flavor without extra calories.

2. Steaming and Boiling

Steaming and boiling are gentle cooking techniques that help retain the natural flavors and nutrients of foods. Use a steamer basket or pot with a lid to steam vegetables, fish, and seafood until tender. Boiling is ideal for cooking grains, legumes, and root vegetables.

Tip: Add herbs, garlic, or onions to the steaming or boiling water to infuse subtle flavors into the food.

3. Sautéing and Stir-Frying

Sautéing and stir-frying are quick cooking methods that use small amounts of oil over high heat. These techniques are perfect for cooking leafy greens, vegetables, and lean meats, preserving their texture and flavor while minimizing added fats.

Tip: Use olive oil or coconut oil for sautéing and stir-frying, as they are heart-healthy fats that add flavor to dishes.

4. Baking and Braising

Baking and braising are slow cooking methods that tenderize tough cuts of meat and infuse flavors into dishes. Use a covered baking dish or Dutch oven to cook meats, vegetables, and grains with a small amount of liquid over low heat for moist and flavorful results.

Tip: Use broth, wine, or citrus juices as braising liquids to add depth and complexity to your dishes.

Mastering these cooking techniques will help you create delicious and nutritious meals that align with the principles of the Atlantic diet. Experiment with different flavors and ingredients to discover new and exciting ways to enjoy Atlantic cuisine.

5. Use Fresh, Seasonal Ingredients

Choose fresh, seasonal ingredients whenever possible. They are often more flavorful and nutrient-dense than their processed counterparts. Visit local markets or farm stands to find the best produce for your meals.

Tip: Plan your meals around seasonal fruits and vegetables to enjoy them at their peak freshness and flavor.

6. Limit Added Fats and Sugars

While the Atlantic diet includes healthy fats from sources like olive oil and nuts, it's important to use them in moderation. Limit the use of added fats and sugars in cooking and opt for natural sweeteners like honey or maple syrup when needed.

Tip: Use herbs, spices, and citrus juices to add flavor to your dishes without relying on added fats and sugars.

7. Practice Portion Control

Pay attention to portion sizes to avoid overeating. Use smaller plates and serving utensils to help control portion sizes and prevent the temptation to overindulge.

Tip: Fill half your plate with vegetables, one-quarter with lean protein, and one-quarter with whole grains for a balanced meal.

8. Experiment with Herbs and Spices

Herbs and spices are key components of the Atlantic diet, adding flavor and aroma to dishes without the need for excess salt, sugar, or fats. Experiment with different herbs and spices to discover new flavor combinations.

Tip: Grow your own herbs in a small garden or on a windowsill for a convenient and cost-effective way to add fresh flavors to your meals.

Incorporating these tips into your cooking routine will help you create delicious and nutritious meals that support your health and well-being. By focusing on fresh, whole foods and mindful cooking practices, you can enjoy the benefits of the Atlantic diet for years to come.

Kitchen Equipment Essentials for the Atlantic Diet

Overview of the importance of having the right kitchen equipment for preparing Atlantic diet meals.

Cutting and Chopping Tools

- Chef's knife: The most versatile knife for chopping vegetables and cutting meat.
- Paring knife: Ideal for peeling and slicing fruits and vegetables.
- Cutting board: Choose a durable and easy-to-clean cutting board.

Cookware

- Skillet or frying pan: Non-stick pans are ideal for cooking with minimal oil.

- Saucepan: Essential for boiling, simmering, and making sauces.

- Stockpot: For preparing soups, stews, and boiling pasta or grains.

Bakeware

- Baking sheet: Use for roasting vegetables or baking fish.

- Casserole dish: Ideal for baking casseroles and gratins.

Food Processor or Blender

- Useful for making sauces, dips, and pureeing ingredients for soups.

Measuring Tools

- Measuring cups and spoons: Essential for accurately measuring ingredients.

Kitchen Utensils

- Wooden spoons: Ideal for stirring and mixing ingredients.
- Spatula: For flipping and serving food.
- Tongs: Useful for handling food while cooking.

Storage Containers

- Containers for storing leftovers and meal prep.

Miscellaneous

- Kitchen scale: Useful for measuring ingredients by weight.
- Citrus juicer: For juicing lemons, limes, and oranges.
- Grater: For grating cheese and vegetables.
- Peeler: For peeling fruits and vegetables.

CHAPTER 6

Incorporating Atlantic Diet Principles into Your Lifestyle

Dining Out on the Atlantic Diet

The Atlantic diet is not just a way of eating at home; it's a lifestyle that can be extended to dining out. Whether you're at a restaurant, café, or social gathering, it's possible to stick to the principles of the Atlantic diet and enjoy delicious, nutritious meals. In this guide, we'll explore how to navigate dining out on the Atlantic diet, from choosing the right restaurant to making healthy choices off the menu.

Choosing the Right Restaurant

When dining out on the Atlantic diet, choosing the right restaurant is key. Look for establishments that offer a variety of fresh, seasonal ingredients and focus on traditional cooking methods. Here are some tips for selecting a restaurant that aligns with the Atlantic diet:

- Locally Sourced Ingredients: Choose restaurants that source their ingredients locally whenever possible. This ensures that you're getting the freshest, most nutritious foods.

- Seafood Selection: Look for restaurants that offer a variety of seafood options, such as salmon, sardines, and mackerel. These are staples of the Atlantic diet and are rich in omega-3 fatty acids.

- Vegetarian Options: Even if you're not vegetarian, choosing restaurants that offer a variety of vegetable-based dishes can help you stick to the Atlantic diet.

- Whole Grains: Restaurants that offer whole grain options, such as brown rice or whole grain bread, are a good choice for Atlantic diet followers.

- Avoiding Processed Foods: Steer clear of restaurants that heavily rely on processed foods and opt for those that focus on whole, natural ingredients.

Making Healthy Choices Off the Menu

Once you've chosen a restaurant, it's time to make healthy choices off the menu. Here are some tips for ordering Atlantic diet-friendly meals:

- Start with Soup or Salad: Begin your meal with a broth-based soup or a salad loaded with fresh vegetables. This can help you control your appetite and get a head start on your vegetable intake.

- Choose Seafood: Look for seafood options that are grilled, baked, or steamed rather than fried. Fish such as salmon, trout, and mackerel are excellent choices.

- Opt for Whole Grains: If possible, choose dishes that include whole grains such as brown rice, quinoa, or whole grain pasta.

- Load Up on Vegetables: Make vegetables the star of your meal by choosing dishes that feature a variety of colorful vegetables.

- Watch Portion Sizes: Many restaurants serve large portion sizes, so consider sharing a meal or asking for a half portion.

- Be Mindful of Sauces and Dressings: Ask for sauces and dressings on the side so you can control how much you consume.

- Hydrate Wisely: Choose water, herbal tea, or other non-caloric beverages instead of sugary drinks or alcohol.

Navigating Social Gatherings

Social gatherings can present challenges when following the Atlantic diet, but with a little planning, you can stay on track. Here are some tips for navigating social gatherings while sticking to the Atlantic diet:

- Plan Ahead: If possible, find out what will be served at the gathering and plan your choices accordingly.

- Offer to Bring a Dish: If you're unsure about the food choices, offer to bring a dish that aligns with the Atlantic diet.

- Eat Before You Go: Have a small, nutritious meal or snack before the gathering so you're not tempted to overindulge.

- Focus on Socializing: Instead of focusing on the food, concentrate on enjoying the company of others.

- Practice Moderation: If there are indulgent foods at the gathering, allow yourself a small portion and savor it mindfully.

Staying Active and Balancing Indulgence

Maintaining an active lifestyle is an important aspect of the Atlantic diet. Incorporating regular physical activity into your routine can help balance out any indulgences you may have while dining out. Here are some tips for staying active:

- Choose Active Social Activities: Instead of meeting friends for a meal, suggest activities that involve movement, such as hiking, biking, or dancing.

- Stay Active Throughout the Day: Look for opportunities to stay active throughout the day, such as taking the stairs instead of the elevator or going for a walk during your lunch break.

- Find Activities You Enjoy: Whether it's yoga, swimming, or playing a sport, finding physical activities you enjoy can make staying active feel like less of a chore.

- Stay Consistent: Aim for at least 150 minutes of moderate-intensity aerobic activity per week, as recommended by health experts.

Managing Special Dietary Needs

If you have special dietary needs or restrictions, dining out on the Atlantic diet may require a bit more planning. Here are some tips for managing special dietary needs while dining out:

- Communicate Your Needs: Don't be afraid to communicate your dietary needs to restaurant staff. Most establishments are willing to accommodate special requests.

- Research Restaurants: Before dining out, research restaurants that are known for catering to special dietary needs, such as vegetarian, gluten-free, or dairy-free options.

- Be Prepared: Consider carrying a small snack or meal replacement bar in case you're unable to find suitable options while dining out.

- Ask Questions: If you're unsure about a dish or its ingredients, don't hesitate to ask your server for more information.

Enjoying the Experience

Above all, remember to enjoy the experience of dining out on the Atlantic diet. Food is not just nourishment for the body; it's also a source of pleasure and enjoyment. By making mindful choices, staying active, and balancing indulgence with healthy habits, you can fully embrace the Atlantic diet lifestyle, even when dining out.

Socializing and Celebrating with Atlantic Diet-Friendly Foods

Social gatherings and celebrations are an integral part of life, and they don't have to derail your commitment to the Atlantic Diet.

With a little planning and creativity, you can enjoy delicious and nutritious meals that align with the principles of the Atlantic Diet while socializing with friends and family.

Planning Ahead

Menu Planning: Before a social event, plan your menu to include Atlantic Diet-friendly dishes that are both nutritious and satisfying. Consider dishes that can be prepared in advance and are easy to serve to a crowd.

Communicate with Hosts: If you're attending an event hosted by someone else, communicate your dietary preferences and restrictions ahead of time. Offer to bring a dish that you can enjoy and share with others.

Atlantic Diet-Friendly Party Foods

Seafood Platter: Create a seafood platter featuring a variety of fresh, local seafood such as shrimp, crab, and fish. Serve with a squeeze of lemon and a side of homemade cocktail sauce made with fresh tomatoes and herbs.

Vegetable Crudité: Prepare a colorful vegetable crudité with an assortment of fresh vegetables such as carrots, bell peppers, cucumbers, and cherry tomatoes. Serve with a homemade hummus or yogurt-based dip.

Whole Grain Bread Basket: Offer a selection of whole grain bread and rolls for guests to enjoy. Serve with a side of olive oil and balsamic vinegar for dipping.

Atlantic Diet-Friendly Desserts: For dessert, consider serving fruit-based desserts such as a fruit salad or a fruit tart made with a whole grain crust. Alternatively, offer small portions of dark chocolate, which is a staple of the Atlantic Diet.

Beverage Options

Water: Provide plenty of water for guests to stay hydrated. Consider infusing water with fresh fruits or herbs for a refreshing twist.

Wine: Offer a selection of red and white wines, which are commonly enjoyed in Atlantic Diet regions. Opt for organic or biodynamic wines when possible.

Herbal Tea: Serve herbal teas such as chamomile or peppermint for a caffeine-free option.

Tips for Enjoying Social Events

Practice Mindful Eating: Take your time to savor each bite and enjoy the flavors and textures of your food.

Focus on the Company: Remember that social gatherings are about more than just the food. Focus on enjoying the company of your friends and family.

Be Flexible: While it's important to stick to the principles of the Atlantic Diet, it's also okay to indulge occasionally. Allow yourself to enjoy small portions of less healthy foods in moderation.

By planning ahead and making thoughtful choices, you can enjoy socializing and celebrating while staying true to the principles of the Atlantic Diet

CHAPTER 7

Maintaining Success on the Atlantic Diet

Staying Motivated

Maintaining Success on the Atlantic Diet: Staying Motivated Congratulations on embarking on the Atlantic diet journey! As you continue on this path to better health and well-being, it's important to stay motivated and committed to your goals. Here are some tips to help you maintain your success on the Atlantic diet:

Setting Realistic Goals

Setting realistic and achievable goals is crucial for staying motivated on the Atlantic diet. Instead of aiming for drastic changes overnight, focus on making small, sustainable changes to your diet and lifestyle. This could be as simple as incorporating more Atlantic diet-friendly foods into your meals each week or gradually reducing your intake of unhealthy foods.

Tracking Your Progress

Keeping track of your progress can help you stay motivated and accountable. Consider keeping a food journal to log your meals and snacks, as well as any changes you notice in your energy levels, mood, or weight. You could also take photos or measurements to visually track your progress over time.

Celebrating Your Successes

Don't forget to celebrate your successes, no matter how small! Whether you've successfully followed the Atlantic diet for a week or you've reached a milestone in your weight loss journey, take the time to acknowledge and celebrate your achievements. This can help boost your motivation and keep you focused on your goals.

Finding Support

Having a strong support system can make a world of difference when it comes to staying motivated on the Atlantic diet. Consider joining a support group or online community where you can connect with others who are following the Atlantic diet. You can share your experiences, ask for advice, and find encouragement when you need it most.

Practicing Mindful Eating

Mindful eating is an important aspect of the Atlantic diet and can help you stay motivated by fostering a deeper connection with your food. Take the time to savor and enjoy each meal, paying attention to the flavors, textures, and aromas. This can help prevent mindless eating and promote a greater appreciation for the food you're eating.

Rewarding Yourself

Rewarding yourself for reaching your goals can be a great way to stay motivated on the Atlantic diet. Treat yourself to something you enjoy, such as a relaxing bath, a new book, or a fun outing with friends. Just make sure your reward aligns with your health goals and doesn't undermine your progress on the Atlantic diet.

Revisiting Your Why

When your motivation starts to wane, take a moment to revisit your why. Why did you decide to start the Atlantic diet? What are your goals and aspirations? Reminding yourself of the reasons behind your dietary choices can reignite your motivation and help you stay committed to your journey.

Embracing Flexibility

While it's important to stay committed to the principles of the Atlantic diet, it's also important to be flexible and adaptable. There may be times when you're faced with challenges or temptations, and that's okay. Instead of viewing these moments as failures, see them as opportunities to learn and grow. Embrace flexibility and focus on making the best choices you can in any given situation.

Seeking Professional Guidance

If you're struggling to stay motivated on the Atlantic diet, consider seeking professional guidance from a registered dietitian or nutritionist. They can provide personalized advice and support to help you overcome any obstacles and stay on track with your goals.

By incorporating these tips into your daily routine, you can stay motivated and committed to your success on the Atlantic diet. Remember, progress takes time, so be patient with yourself and celebrate each step forward on your journey to better health and wellness.

Tips for overcoming common challenges

Overcoming Common Challenges on the Atlantic Diet

Following the Atlantic diet can be a rewarding experience, but like any lifestyle change, it comes with its own set of challenges. Here are some tips to help you overcome common obstacles and stay on track:

- Finding Fresh Seafood: Look for local fish markets or seafood counters at grocery stores. Ask the staff for recommendations on the freshest options and how to prepare them.
- Dealing with Seasonal Availability: Embrace seasonal produce and seafood. Plan your meals around what's available, and experiment with new ingredients to keep things interesting.
- Budget Constraints: Shop smart by buying in bulk, opting for frozen seafood when fresh is too expensive, and choosing cheaper cuts of meat. Look for sales and discounts on fruits, vegetables, and whole grains.

- Time Constraints: Meal prep is your friend. Spend a few hours each week chopping vegetables, cooking grains, and preparing proteins so you can quickly assemble meals during the week.

- Social Situations: Communicate your dietary preferences to friends and family. Offer to bring a dish to gatherings that aligns with the Atlantic diet, or eat beforehand so you're not tempted by unhealthy options.

- Cravings for Unhealthy Foods: Find Atlantic diet-friendly alternatives to your favorite unhealthy foods. For example, swap out chips for roasted nuts or indulge in dark chocolate instead of candy.

- Lack of Variety: Explore new recipes and ingredients to keep your meals exciting. Look for inspiration in cookbooks, online resources, and local restaurants that focus on Mediterranean cuisine.

- Dining Out Challenges: Look for restaurants that offer seafood and vegetable-focused dishes. Don't be afraid to ask for modifications to suit your dietary needs.

- Plateauing Weight Loss: Mix up your exercise routine and pay attention to portion sizes. Consider consulting with a nutritionist or dietitian for personalized advice.
- Lack of Support: Join online forums or social media groups focused on the Atlantic diet. Share your experiences and learn from others who are on a similar journey.

By being proactive and creative, you can overcome these challenges and make the Atlantic diet a sustainable and enjoyable part of your lifestyle.

FAQs about the Atlantic Diet

What is the Atlantic Diet?

The Atlantic Diet is a dietary pattern inspired by the traditional eating habits of countries bordering the Atlantic Ocean, such as Portugal, Spain, France, and parts of the UK. It emphasizes fresh, seasonal, and locally sourced foods.

What are the key principles of the Atlantic Diet?

The key principles of the Atlantic Diet include a high consumption of fruits, vegetables, whole grains, fish, and seafood, along with moderate amounts of dairy, poultry, and eggs. It also encourages the use of olive oil as the primary source of fat and limits the intake of red meat and processed foods.

Is the Atlantic Diet similar to the Mediterranean Diet?

Yes, the Atlantic Diet shares many similarities with the Mediterranean Diet, including an emphasis on plant-based foods, seafood, and olive oil. However, the Atlantic Diet also includes foods specific to the Atlantic region, such as certain types of fish and seaweed.

What are some typical foods in the Atlantic Diet?

Typical foods in the Atlantic Diet include fish (such as cod, sardines, and mackerel), seafood (such as shrimp and clams), fruits (such as oranges and apples), vegetables (such as kale and cabbage), whole grains (such as oats and barley), and legumes (such as beans and lentils).

Is the Atlantic Diet suitable for vegetarians or vegans?

Yes, the Atlantic Diet can be adapted to suit vegetarian or vegan diets by focusing on plant-based sources of protein, such as legumes, nuts, and seeds, and incorporating dairy alternatives, such as almond milk or soy yogurt.

Can I lose weight on the Atlantic Diet?

The Atlantic Diet can be a healthy way to lose weight, as it emphasizes whole, nutrient-dense foods and limits processed foods and added sugars. However, individual weight loss results may vary depending on factors such as calorie intake and physical activity level.

Are there any health benefits associated with the Atlantic Diet?

Yes, the Atlantic Diet has been associated with several health benefits, including a reduced risk of heart disease, stroke, and certain types of cancer. It may also help improve cholesterol levels and blood sugar control.

How can I incorporate the Atlantic Diet into my daily life?

You can incorporate the Atlantic Diet into your daily life by focusing on whole, minimally processed foods, cooking with olive oil, and enjoying a variety of fruits, vegetables, fish, and seafood.

It's also important to stay hydrated and limit the intake of sugary beverages and snacks.

Are there any specific cooking techniques used in the Atlantic Diet?

Yes, the Atlantic Diet often involves simple cooking techniques, such as grilling, baking, and steaming, to preserve the natural flavors of foods. Olive oil is commonly used for sautéing and dressing salads.

Can I eat out while following the Atlantic Diet?

Yes, you can eat out while following the Atlantic Diet. Look for restaurants that offer fresh seafood, vegetable-based dishes, and whole grain options. Avoid fried foods and dishes high in saturated fats.

Is alcohol allowed on the Atlantic Diet?

In moderation, alcohol, particularly red wine, is allowed on the Atlantic Diet. However, it's important to consume alcohol responsibly and in moderation.

How does the Atlantic Diet compare to other popular diets, such as the Mediterranean Diet or the DASH Diet?

While there are similarities between the Atlantic Diet, Mediterranean Diet, and DASH Diet (Dietary Approaches to Stop Hypertension), each diet has its own unique focus and guidelines. The Atlantic Diet emphasizes foods commonly found in Atlantic coastal regions.

Are there any specific health conditions that the Atlantic Diet can help manage or prevent?

The Atlantic Diet is associated with a reduced risk of cardiovascular diseases, including heart disease and stroke. It may also help improve cholesterol levels, blood pressure, and blood sugar control.

Is the Atlantic Diet sustainable for long-term health and weight management?

Yes, the Atlantic Diet can be sustainable for long-term health and weight management, as it promotes a balanced and varied diet rich in nutrients and low in processed foods.

Are there any cultural or social aspects to the Atlantic Diet?

Yes, the Atlantic Diet is often linked to cultural traditions and social gatherings, where meals are seen as a time to connect with family and friends. Sharing meals and enjoying local, seasonal foods are important aspects of the diet.

CONCLUSION

As you conclude your journey through the Atlantic diet, it's important to reflect on the key principles and benefits of this dietary pattern. Throughout this book, we've explored the rich culinary traditions of the Atlantic coastal regions and delved into the health benefits of the Atlantic diet.

Understanding the Atlantic Diet

We started by understanding the fundamentals of the Atlantic diet, which is inspired by the traditional eating habits of countries bordering the Atlantic Ocean. This diet emphasizes fresh, seasonal, and locally sourced foods, along with the moderate consumption of dairy, poultry, and eggs.

Key Principles and Guidelines

The key principles of the Atlantic diet include a high intake of fruits, vegetables, whole grains, fish, and seafood, as well as the use of olive oil as the primary source of fat. This diet also limits the consumption of red meat and processed foods, promoting a balanced and nutrient-rich approach to eating.

Benefits of the Atlantic Diet

One of the main benefits of the Atlantic diet is its positive impact on health. Studies have shown that the Atlantic diet can reduce the risk of heart disease, stroke, and certain types of cancer. It can also improve cholesterol levels, blood pressure, and blood sugar control.

Incorporating the Atlantic Diet into Your Lifestyle

To incorporate the Atlantic diet into your lifestyle, focus on whole, minimally processed foods, and cook with olive oil. Enjoy a variety of fruits, vegetables, fish, and seafood, and stay hydrated. Eating out is also possible while following the Atlantic diet, as long as you choose restaurants that offer Atlantic diet-friendly options.

Sustainability and Long-Term Success

The Atlantic diet is not just a short-term diet but a sustainable way of eating for long-term health and well-being. By embracing the principles of the Atlantic diet, you can enjoy a balanced and varied diet that promotes overall health and longevity.

Final Thoughts and Encouragement

As you continue your journey with the Atlantic diet, remember that every meal is an opportunity to nourish your body and honor the culinary traditions of the Atlantic coastal regions. Stay true to your goals, be kind to yourself, and enjoy the abundance of flavors and nutrients that the Atlantic diet has to offer.

Thank you for embarking on this journey with me. Here's to your health, happiness, and continued success with the Atlantic diet!

Made in the USA
Las Vegas, NV
01 June 2024

90607018R00103